Via Roma

Via Roma

The History of Rome in Fifty Streets

Willemijn Van Dijk

Robert Naborn
translator

BAYLOR UNIVERSITY PRESS

Originally published by Ambo | Anthos
Uitgevers, Amsterdam

First published in English in 2018 by Baylor University Press,
Waco, Texas 76798.

Cover Design by Aaron Cobbs, Baylor University Press.
Cover Art: Map of Rome, Italy, issued by Magro. Leonard
(Leonardo Bufalini), *Roma*, 1551–1560.

The English translation has been cataloged by the Library of
Congress under ISBN 978-1-4813-0905-9.

Printed in the United States of America on acid-free paper
with a minimum of 30 percent post-consumer waste
recycled content.

CONTENTS

INTRODUCTION

HOW IS A CITY BORN?

> *"For, although Rome in its entirety is in ruins, nothing, even completely unblemished, compares to her."*
>
> —Master Gregory, a twelfth-century visitor to Rome[1]

How is a city born? Most guidebooks will tell you that Rome was founded on April 21, 753 BCE. This suspiciously precise fact has often been blindly copied; do not even the Romans themselves commemorate the founding of their city every year on April 21? No one seems to have given any thought to the absurd notion that a city can be founded on a certain day. Of course, there are examples of colonies that were founded from scratch, but even in those cases the actual founding was more of a historical process than a historical event. Rome was not a colony, and it was not built in one day. The mythical character of many of the stories surrounding the founding of the *caput mundi* hint at that: there was no Rome on April 21, 753 BCE.

That is, there was no city of Rome yet. The tradition of naming 753 as the year of its founding is a fabrication dating back to antiquity, and apparently based on a miscalculation to boot.

When can a place actually be called a city? This is a question archaeologists might struggle with, too. When does a cluster of huts become a village, and when does this village become a city? For the period preceding the

[1] Magistri Gregorii, *The Marvels of Rome* (*Mirabilia Urbis Romae*), ed. and trans. Francis Morgan Nichols, 2nd ed. with new introduction, gazetteer, and bibliography by Eileen Gardiner (New York, 1986).

keeping of official city rights documents in national archives, archaeologists rely on material remains of a community: they will look for the earliest evidence, preferably in stone, of a communal construction project with monumental proportions. But is there nothing that precedes that? Is it possible to recognize characteristics of a city when a first sense of community emerges that drives people's actions—the collective defense of home and hearth, the start of commercial activity in the form of a local market?

Although a sense of community is undeniably important as the requirement for the genesis of a city, it is, of course, impossible to find a "feeling" in the archaeological records. Unfortunately, there are almost no written records available for the earliest period of cultivation and activities that would allow us to read such an awareness of community into the utterly insignificant Rome of the eighth century BCE—not from that time itself in any case. From excavations we know that Rome is older than most ancient Roman historians thought it was: the earliest traces of habitation date back to before 1000 BCE. Although historians and archaeologists still know very little about this small city on the Tiber River, burgeoning during the Italic Iron Age (the early first millennium BCE), it is possible to get an idea of its genesis by looking beyond its founding myth about Romulus, Remus, and the she-wolf. The story is still fascinating, but from the start, it clearly tries to put Rome in the center of the world.

A community does not simply come into being. It will first show itself when a group of people (think they) have something in common and simultaneously feel that they are significantly different from members of other groups. The notion is rational, in that a community defines its own entity by virtue of one or more oppositional groups against which they can rebel or with whom they can compare themselves. It would perhaps be better to take an unimpeded look at history, a panoramic 360 degrees. After all, where exactly was the cradle of the eternal city located? What was the world like when Rome came into being?

With this question my journey through the streets of the Eternal City starts. On my walk from the Tiber into the city, I will ask myself what story each marble street sign is hiding and which piece of the puzzle of Rome's vast heritage it holds, from its founding up until today. The uniform signs—which have only had more or less "permanent" street names since 1798—are somehow reassuring, allowing some purchase on what at first glance comes across as an elusive historic labyrinth.

Nearly every visitor to Rome in the past two thousand years has bemoaned the overwhelming presence of the innumerous monuments and art treasures, and the at-times overpowering layers of history concealed behind each stone. "What is required when in Rome," Dutch author and antiquity lover Louis Couperus says in his 1894 travel diary, "is first, to know your history facts inside-and-out—both world and art history—from Romulus to Bernini; also to be well versed in Rome's topographies . . . for example, when you enter St. Peter's, you should be instantly reminded of the Circus of Nero and the Basilica of Constantine."[2]

Visitors to Rome encounter not only monuments and thousands of layers of history but also countless myths, anecdotes, and folktales circling like hovering ghosts around those tangible remnants of ancient, medieval, renaissance, and baroque Rome. Stories swirl about crazy emperors and popes and their compliant victims, about hopeless love and ghastly crimes, about archangels and demons, and about the rivalry between Bernini and Borromini, which has reportedly even been immortalized in marble. I make my way through centuries of folklore and mythmaking, and, using the marble signs as my arbitrarily meandering guide, I search for the

[2] Louis Couperus, *Reis-impressies*, Stichting Volledige Werken Louis Couperus (Utrecht/Antwerpen, 1990).

true story of the history of Rome—the only city in the world where everybody understands that, when you simply say *urbs* ("the city"), you are talking about Rome. "I am not sure if it will be worth the effort to describe the history of the Roman people, from the beginnings of the city. I am not certain, and if I did know, I would not presume to say so, because I realize that the story is not only ancient, but also very well known." With these words Livy begins his magnum opus, *Ab urbe condita* ("From the founding of the City"),[3] which he wrote in the first century BCE. More than two thousand years of history separate us from Titus Livius. Nowhere have I found better, more fitting words to begin a history of Rome.

History is never finished, so, by definition, one cannot write a comprehensive history of Rome. The squares and streets set the rhythm and direction in this book, mercilessly speeding past countless historical events and characters that remain unexplored. In the spirit of Livy's opening words, my aim is merely to share with you my never-ending interest in and love for Rome and to honor the Eternal City in my own, self-effacing way.

Just like many others who have tried to write about the history of Rome, I am an outsider. I was a teenager when my schooling brought me to Rome for the first time. At age sixteen I boarded the train to Italy. When I arrived at the Stazione Termini in Rome, I felt a kind of euphoria, much like the feeling Goethe describes in his diary on November 1, 1786: "Yes, I have finally arrived in this capital of the world!" When my feet first touched Roman soil I felt that Rome was a place unlike any I had ever visited before. I solemnly promised myself one thing: that I would be back, alone, to stay for a longer period of time. I did come back, with a scholarship and a mountain of expectations. I kept coming back after that. It was the beginning of an exploration without

[3] Livy, *The Rise of Rome, Books 1–5*, trans. T. J. Luce, Oxford World's Classics (New York, 2008).

a destination; a continuous familiarization with the many faces of Rome. Today, the city still exceeds my impossibly high expectations.

Although humbled by the greatness of all my predecessors, when reading Livy's words I sense I can relate to him in at least one way—by feeling the joy and fulfillment of contributing to the preservation of the memory of Rome, street by street, square by square. I know of no greater pleasure than to wander through the streets of Rome. As I take you by the hand, I invite you to join me in discovering this pleasure. Let's start at the Tiber.

I

THE TIBER

LOOKING FOR THE CRADLE OF ROME

The banks of the Tiber are the closest you can physically get to the birthplace of Rome. For the earliest signs of the first group of huts that would grow into the Eternal City, we follow the only "road" that we know with certainty was already there in the eighth century BCE, and even way before that: the river that meanders right through the center of Rome. The first time I saw that powerful river flowing ferociously below me, I was on the Ponte Garibaldi—although at the time I did not know the name of that bridge nor the rest of the city at all.

I often think back to those very first times I wandered through Rome. Not knowing the way, I roamed the city feeling disoriented. It reinforced the impression those countless monuments and ruins made on me. Now I know every bend in the river, but at that time I had the feeling the Tiber kept popping up everywhere I went. Standing on the Ponte Garibaldi, I remember being mesmerized, both by the idea that I was face-to-face with the river where it all began and by the bizarrely shaped island that lay before me.

Almost every scholar considers the Tiber one of the most (and possibly *the* most) important factor in giving Rome the strength to set itself apart and eventually rise above its neighbors. And there were enough neighbors who, archaeologically speaking, were more prominent in this early phase than the "Romans." As far as we know, there were Etruscans in the north; Sabines, Volsci, Hernici, and Aequi in the east; and Greek colonists in the south. The place from which Rome would spring was within Latium, the territory of the

Latins: a ford over the river Tiber, where nowadays you can find that strangely shaped island that provided a permanent strategic advantage to the first peasants who settled there. It allowed those peasants not only to guard the river crossing but also to profit from its location on the intersection of some Italic roads that were already well traveled during the Iron Age. From east to west ran an important salt route, commemorated to this day by the Via Salaria (*sale* = salt). Through the mouth of the Tiber, the precious salt was transported inland from the salt ponds on the coast. Anxious peasants and shepherds would have waited at the foot of the Apennines for the "white gold" with which they conserved hides, meat, and other perishables. On the spot from which Rome would later emerge, the salt route crossed the most important north-south route in Italy, which ran from Magna Graecia in the south (so called because it was for the most part colonized by the Greeks), to the Etruscan territory in the north, roughly in current Tuscany.

The differing emphases of current and ancient historians who wrote about the birth of Rome may be telling—both sets of assertions are true but are influenced by their zeitgeist. Historians today emphasize above all the commercial advantages of the ford over the Tiber, while historians of ancient Rome, especially those from the period of the late Republic (first century BCE), highlighted the strategic military advantages and even moral advantages in their analyses. For example, Cicero (106–43 BCE) wrote that the location had been chosen because it was a sheltered, easily defended spot, one not directly by the sea where dangers such as attacks from foreign nations and piracy were always lurking (and with that also the danger of moral decay). One of the first of the seven hills around the Tiber to be inhabited, the Palatine, also offered a well-defendable position.

The western slope of the Palatine, where the foot of the hill almost touches the water of the Tiber, is where the earliest inhabitants—let's call them proto-Romans for now—become archaeologically visible for the first time. Here archaeologists found the remains of groups of huts from the ninth and eighth centuries BCE, indicating the existence of clustering villages that did not differ much from other settlements in the surrounding hilly landscape. These remains did not appear out of thin air: finds of pottery in the Tiber valley date back to the tenth and in some cases even the fourteenth century BCE. In the eighth century, there were small repositories near clusters of huts. These repositories were filled with sacrifices, a possible indication of early forms of collective ritual activities. This may not sound all that thrilling, but it is a first archaeological indicator of solidarity. Religious acts were apparently no longer limited to family groups that lived in the clusters of huts led by their own head of the family; they were now actually celebrated with neighbors, too, in meeting places that were considered sacred.

In the graves that were discovered in the area around the huts (in addition to the Palatine, on the Velia and on the Quirinal), in the valley where tourists now admire the remains of the Forum Romanum, archaeologists mainly found lots of pottery, but also bronze objects. The contents of the graves showed a strong resemblance to the objects given to accompany the dead in many other places in central Italy during this period. Some graves contained more luxury and prestige objects than others, so we may assume there were differences in wealth and (social) status. Moreover, two distinct burial rituals were apparent: *fossa* and *pozzo* graves, that is, trenches in which to bury bodies (inhumation), and pits in which to bury cinerary urns (cremation), respectively. Archaeologists generally assume that different burial rituals represent separate groups of people, in this particular case perhaps a number of separate hillside villages.

The farming community that settled on the Tiber's banks seems to have lived in a typical village for this time period and region in Italy, with inhabitants that made use of local earthenware: the dark, matte, and often robust *bucchero* vases. Between the Palatine and the Tiber, on what would later be called the Forum Boarium, earthenware was also found, suggesting an open attitude toward the outside world. On the banks of the especially well-positioned trading route that was the Tiber, earthenware was traded both from the Greek settlement in Italy and from overseas. Evidence has also been found for the existence of a cult of Hercules, the patron of shepherds and merchants. Scholars surmise that Phoenician merchants, among whom Hercules was known as Melqart, introduced the worship of Hercules here. All in all, it seems that the Forum Boarium had already grown into a kind of a marketplace during the emergence phase of the settlement on the Tiber: a place of exchange and of short and long distance trade.

To sum up, what we have is a small village on the Palatine Hill, inhabited by subsistence farmers and perhaps a few shepherds, and some neighboring villages on the Quirinal, Capitoline, and Velia Hills (where archaeologically comparable remains have been found dating back to the ninth and eighth centuries BCE). These proto-Romans worked their land, kept livestock, and perhaps shared their meadows with a few shepherds. The hillside villagers had a communal cemetery and a marketplace, through which they were in contact with faraway places. There were differences in wealth and status; the villagers did not live in an entirely egalitarian community. The only apparent collective events were certain cult activities, rituals during which sacrificial artifacts were deposited.

The *other* story of the birth of Rome is, with its exact date (April 21, 753 BCE) and exciting plot (a she-wolf and two brothers, Romulus and Remus, who hate each other), perhaps more attractive, but what I have described above is, in a few paragraphs, the actual way in which a world power was born: slowly but steadily, and, frankly, not so extraordinarily. The process was not very romantic, but even Livy, who described the founding legend of Romulus and Remus both extensively and engagingly in his *Ab urbe condita*, had to admit that Rome had actually started out "small and insignificant."

In fact, tourists today cannot really touch nascent Rome anywhere anymore. In the clutter of centuries-old archaeological remains and green trees on the Palatine, laypeople will have a hard time finding evidence of the oldest Rome, and even if they succeed in making sense of all those centuries overlapping each other, they will not easily find themselves face-to-face with a tangible object from the earliest days of Rome. It is mostly the monumental edifices from the Imperial Period, built centuries later, whose skeletons are still visible lying across the Palatine. The huts of Rome's first inhabitants, from which only post holes remain, have become overgrown, both literally and figuratively, and built over. Down below, on the Forum Boarium, you can no longer find visible remains from Rome's earliest history either. The temples on that forum are some of the earliest monuments still standing in Rome, but they were not built by the first peasants. Only in its name does the Forum Boarium (meaning "cattle market") still remind us of the commercial role it played in Rome's earliest days.

There is only one tangible, visible, touchable, and audible element that has defied the nearly three thousand years that separate us from primordial Romans: the Tiber. Back then it flowed freely—and therefore also frequently overflowed. Nowadays it is neatly dammed in and subject to the will of the city—just as half the world would be, during the heyday of the Roman Empire that lay ahead.

II

VIA MONTE TARPEO

THE FIRST BETRAYAL OF THE CITY

The narrow road zigzags upward on the southern slope of the Capitoline Hill. The Via Monte Tarpeo is actually rather hidden, but no street in the center of Rome is safe from tourism. When we climb the Via Monte Tarpeo, on our way to one of the most beautiful vistas of Rome, Segways pass us left and right. This is the only road to the top of the Capitoline Hill that can be negotiated on two wheels. Walking up is harder, but the effort makes the reward waiting at the top even sweeter.

It is not known when the custom began, but once at the top of the Via Monte Tarpeo, people turn their backs and throw coins, targeting the architrave a few feet below the banister. On this spot, it would be better to face the Forum Romanum. This is especially true when dusk falls in springtime, when the view of the old valley, with the majestic Colosseum in the background, is most breathtaking. Walking down below, among the fragments of Roman history, you might easily get discouraged, and the cluttered layers of history might make it nearly impossible to imagine what this place was like long ago. But from the Via Monte Tarpeo you get a clearer view. With the ruins at your feet, it is as if everything is coming to life before your eyes, as if pillars, remnants of walls, streets, arches, and remains of temples are melting together into a perfectly coherent ensemble. This is the coherent ensemble—the long-lost and ruinous promise of limitless power (*imperium sine fine*).

How did the group of hillside villages on the Tiber transition into a small city? How did a valley full of graves morph into the vibrant center of that city? The upward-circling Via Monte Tarpeo points precisely to this "transition period" with which past and present historians still grapple. The Mons Tarpeius is mentioned by a number of Roman authors—Varro, Livy, and Suetonius, for instance—as the "original name" of the Capitoline Hill. It sometimes signifies the entire hill, at other times only the southwestern corner. The Roman historiographers and chroniclers all wrote about this corner of the Capitoline Hill, due to its connection to a rather gruesome old Roman custom. The "Tarpeian Rock" (its names in Latin range from *mons*, *arx*, and *saxum* to *rupes*) in the southwest corner was the place from which, before an anxiously waiting crowd, "criminals were flung," as the Greek author Plutarch dryly and casually notes in his *Life of Sulla* (1.3).

No spot in ancient Rome was chosen by chance; every place name hides a centuries-old story—at least, that is what the Roman authors want us to believe. According to them, the execution rock was named after one of the most notorious traitors in the city's history, a greedy individual and a disgrace to everything Rome stood for. This primordial criminal from the earliest history of the city was, of course, a woman, and her name was Tarpeia. A seemingly pious and innocent person, Tarpeia was a priestess of the goddess Vesta. She, a so-called Vestal Virgin and daughter of the Roman commander Spurius Tarpeius, had made a strict chastity vow. The leader of the neighboring Sabines, Titus Tatius, wanted to seize the fledgling Roman city, and he managed to bribe Tarpeia with gold, despite her chaste reputation. He needed her help so that his soldiers could storm the fortified Capitoline Hill, where the Roman troops were entrenched. Tarpeia fulfilled her promise and smuggled the enemy inside—after which she was immediately killed by the Sabines (she was supposedly crushed to death by the shields of the enemy she had personally invited in).

Everyone reading or hearing this story, including the Romans in the days of the Republic and the Empire, knows the outcome: in the end Rome was victorious. Even in these earliest confrontations with neighboring peoples, the Romans emerged as victors every time—this much of the story is undeniably true. The Sabines were overcome, and the Romans found the body of the traitor who had taken them to the brink of defeat: Tarpeia. They flung her body from the rock, which would bear her name from then on. The first Roman laws, drawn up in the fifth century BCE, said that from now on traitors and other criminals were to undergo the same fate as Tarpeia. Based on documents and on oral tradition, we know that the last criminal was thrown from the Tarpeian Rock in 43 CE; the punishment was outlawed after that. The name Mons Tarpeius must have survived for quite awhile—it reappears in an inscription halfway through the third century, and in the current street name, Via Monte Tarpeo.

The story of Tarpeia came to us through two men who were born in the first century BCE: the poet Propertius and the historian Livy. Just like countless other stories about the period immediately following the founding of Rome, it has a legendary character—after all, it happened centuries ago. The stories represent elegant solutions to a problem that not only the Roman historiographers but also their successors have run into: nobody knows exactly how a collection of peasant villages transitioned into the small, ambitious city of Rome. Written documentation, handed down or not, does not appear until the end of the sixth century BCE, after the consecration of the temple of Jupiter Optimus Maximus and the creation of the Republic. All we can say with certainty about the small sixth-century city of Rome is that in appearance and organization it did not substantially differ from its contemporary Greek counterparts, which were also aristocracies.

The quest to fill this lacuna, by Livy for instance, has led to the creation of a so-called "Regal Period," a time span of more than two centuries (from 753 to 509 BCE) in which a king (*rex*, plural *reges*) was always the leader of the city. Livy came up with seven in all, and to those seven kings, several religious, political, administrative, and military initiatives were attributed, which laid the groundwork for what was becoming a "serious" city. The story lines, which include, in addition to the story about Tarpeia, the famous rape of the Sabine women, are dismissed today as fascinating fabrications and the result of an imaginative and meaningful oral tradition.

Of course, archaeologists have searched underground for sixth-century BCE Rome—the early Roman kingdom—and they have been able cautiously to establish that during that time Rome was indeed slowly growing and probably becoming more powerful than its small neighboring city-states. That overlaps at least in part with the period that ancient authors identify as the Regal Period. It is difficult to tell what happened in the run-up to that sixth century, the era of Livy's first three kings. Based on what archaeologists have found, Rome still resembled any other place in central Italy and even beyond. Any significant differences that could be mentioned would be to the detriment of the emerging city on the Tiber: in Etruria, and also south of Rome, there were places that were much richer and boasted more urban structures and a much more distinguished aristocratic elite. Social hierarchy was certainly present in seventh-century Rome, as can be seen in the cache of bronze weaponry in a tomb on the Esquiline, but it would only later develop into a more complex structure. It may always remain a mystery how Rome managed to rise above its neighbors. It is certainly not a given that the development was linear; there must have been ups and downs. A possible course of events is that farming techniques improved, commerce flourished, the population increased, and the hillside villages simply grew together. This way, an increase in collective endeavors—defense, commerce, rituals, cults—would happen almost as a matter of course.

The first confirmation of a collective, "urban" awareness is seen sometime during the period 650–575 BCE, when the populace drained and tamped down the swampy valley that would later become the Forum Romanum. Thus the road was quite literally paved for a new phase in the early history of Rome. To grow from a small group of villages into a small city, Rome actually did not have to do much more than expand and merge. However, to grow from a small city into a world power, it needed more: a little help from outside, for starters.

III

VIA DEL VELABRO

THE ETRUSCANS IN ROME

It is certain that Rome was built on hills (whether the hills numbered seven is disputed). Not only archaeological evidence but also the (scanty) written documentation points in that direction. The sources mention *montani*—"mountain dwellers." According to the author Sextus Pompeius Festus (second century CE), the *montani* celebrated an annual feast or ritual called Septimontium in the earliest days of Rome, which seems to confirm that Rome was indeed built on seven hills. If you could zoom out and disregard the current borders, you would be able to see those hills were situated in the area between Latium and Etruria (roughly present-day Tuscany). Just north of the Tiber lay the border with the territory of Veii, an Etruscan city. It is not inconceivable that the earliest inhabitants of Rome consisted of a hodgepodge of Latins, Etruscans, and, for example, Sabines.

One of the few places in Rome that features a reference to the city's supposed Etruscan past is the Via del Velabro. It is a small, forlorn, and insignificant street, sloppily winding between the Palatine and the Capitoline hills. But the street name hides a distant and long-lost past. Velabro, or Velabrum, is the ancient name of the valley between the Forum Romanum and the Forum Boarium. The name was probably derived from Etruscan. Wandering across today's Via del Velabro we stumble upon the San Giorgio in Velabro, a very old church that was built under Pope Leo II (682–683) but that was not consecrated to San Giorgio until the pontificate of Greek Pope Zachary (741–752). This small church was not the first building on this spot—it was built on the foundations of a small dwelling of Greek monks, which in turn rested on Roman remains. Louis Couperus' complaint in his *Letter from Rome* about how much historical knowledge was required of one visiting Rome rings true here, too: the famed layering of the city can be found in its most obscure corners. Nearby a more tangible reminder of antiquity is still proudly standing. Despite its good condition, this arch escapes the attention of most passersby. It is the *arcus constantini*, better known as the Arch of Janus (Quadrifrons), the two-headed god who was patron of all doors and gates and after whom our first month of the year was named. The arch was probably erected for the Emperor Constantine by his son and successor Constantius II.

In the earliest days of Rome, the Vicus Tuscus, or "Etruscan Street," ran straight across the Velabrum valley. It connected the Forum Romanum and the Forum Boarium, the cattle market. Today only the first section of the Vicus Tuscus can still be seen, between the temple of Castor and Pollux and the Basilica Julia on the forum. From there the Etruscan Street more or less followed the course of the current Via San Teodoro, up until the San Giorgio in Velabro. Varro, Livy, and Tacitus all came up with different origins of the name Vicus Tuscus—the Tusci were allies of Romulus who settled in the valley, or Etruscan refugees, or guest workers who had come to Rome for the construction of the first temples. What all these stories have in common is that they try to find an explanation for what may remain forever unclear: why did the Etruscans come to Rome (or had they always been there?), and why did they live in this particular part of the city?

Not only the hills numbered seven. Seven was also the number of kings that reigned over early Rome, according to Roman tradition. Historically, the first four, Romulus, Numa Pompilius, Tullus Hostilius, and Ancus Marcius, were obscure figures, in the sense that they seem to be mostly legendary fantasies. Of course this does not mean that the development of Rome stagnated during the periods when they allegedly reigned (the eighth and seventh centuries BCE).

All evidence suggests that the last three kings, Tarquinius Priscus, Servius Tullius, and Tarquinius Superbus, were of Etruscan origin. Their reigns cover nearly the entire sixth century BCE, marking the period in which Rome manifested as a city or small city-state for the first time. The draining and paving of the Forum Romanum point in that direction, but also a first rampart was built, on the Esquiline, and the first temples were erected. These temples followed the Etruscan building tradition, and they were decorated with terracotta statues painted in bright colors. Etruscan earthenware, the dark-grey and glossy *bucchero*, is found very frequently during this time period. The existence of a Velabrum valley and an "Etruscan Street" is, in this context, actually not at all puzzling.

IV

VIA DEL TEMPIO DI GIOVE

THE LAST KING

Around 500 BCE, the Regal Period came to an end. The end of an era, of a certain form of government—how does that work? According to later historians, especially Livy, the last king, Tarquin, or Lucius Tarquinius Superbus, was dethroned by Lucius Junius Brutus in 509 BCE. The direct cause was a family scandal: the rape of a pious girl, Lucretia, by Tarquin's son Sextus. If the story is true, then this incident must not have been more than the straw that broke the camel's back. The power of the Roman kings was absolute, but by then they were always advised—and were themselves appointed—by a council of elders, occupied by the heads of the most distinguished aristocratic families of Rome: the Senate (derived from *senex*, Latin for "old man"). There was a reason for Tarquin's nickname: Superbus, "the Haughty" or "the Proud One." Modern-day historians assume that the Tarquinii were not ousted simply because of cruelties and scandals, but also because Tarquin had shown little interest in the respected advisory body and because senators (such as Brutus) felt they weren't listened to anymore.

That is how rebellion could rear its head among the patricians, the members of the aristocratic upper layer that had manifested more and more in the course of the sixth century BCE. The patricians saw their influence diminish under Superbus in favor of the king's power. Of course, the king did not encourage the splintering of power: he would benefit from treating his subjects as a collective, the Roman community. An example of this mindset is when Tarquin had a great temple built in Rome dedicated to Jupiter, the chief deity of all Romans. More precisely, Tarquin was the one who completed it: construction had begun under Tarquinius Priscus. The temple of Jupiter, *il tempio di Giove*, had three niches (*cellae*): in the middle that of the Roman chief deity himself, on both sides the *cellae* for his wife Juno and his daughter Minerva. If you are looking for the origin of the Romans, you have to ask whether there is anything left of this oldest temple, the most ancient symbol of the "Romanitas." A modern Roman street bearing Jupiter's name, the Via del Tempio di Giove, gives a hint about the original location of the temple.

Although the Via del Tempio di Giove marks the spot where the temple used to stand long ago, to really experience it we have to leave the road and enter the Capitoline Museums. In the Esedra di Marco Aurelio, a relatively new museum hall, we find the impressive blocks of stone that once formed the foundations of the famous temple for Jupiter Optimus Maximus. As described by Pliny, Livy, and Cicero, among others, the temple was rebuilt, embellished, and renovated countless times through the centuries (according to sources, the temple even burned to the ground in 83 BCE), but that does not diminish the uniqueness of these foundation walls—which, in themselves, aren't very beautiful to look at. They take you back to when Rome was a substantial local power with an impressive territory. But considering what was to come, Rome was still only in its infancy.

When the king and his family were ousted, the rebels established a Republic. A new distribution of power was needed. The most important matters the king had always handled were commanding the troops, jurisdiction, and leading rituals. The political power, the actual governing of Rome, passed to two magistrates after the abolition of the monarchy. About a century and a half later, these magistrates would become known as consuls (*consules*). Although they enjoyed almost the same power as the former kings, it was a limited power: consuls could veto each other's plans and could only hold office for one year. During this year they were inviolable in many ways, but afterward they could still be held accountable for any misdeeds during their term. They were assisted by two *quaestors*, supervisors of the Treasury. Both the Senate and the people's assembly (the origins of both groups are not entirely known, but they certainly already existed as institutions) remained the most important advisory bodies, and the influence of the Senate—the council of old men—only increased. So in the end it was not the king but the first republican leaders who consecrated the temple of Jupiter on the Capitoline Hill when the temple was finally finished at the end of the sixth century BCE.

The temple of Jupiter Optimus Maximus developed into the center of the Roman state cult not only during the Republic but also during the later Imperial Period (beginning in 27 BCE). In early Rome, religion, a concept that is always contextually, historically, and culturally charged, had an exceptional significance that was much more public and political than we can envision today. Public offerings were brought to the temple in the name of the consuls or, later, the emperor. For military leaders returning from the battlefield, Jupiter's temple on the Capitoline was the final leg of an official triumphal march through Rome. The temple also acted as a repository of important archival records and prestigious state assets. Over the centuries, the pace of the Roman Empire's growth only increased. The acquired riches resulted in this primordial sanctuary being continuously embellished and renovated, allowing the Capitoline temple to become the symbol of the power and invulnerability of Rome.

V

PIAZZA DEI CINQUECENTO

A WALL FOR THE FLEDGLING REPUBLIC

How many travelers arriving by train in Rome will ask themselves: is *this* the Eternal City? Regardless of whether they have taken the train all the way from home or the Leonardo Express from Fiumicino airport, for almost everyone Rome begins at Stazione Termini and the Piazza dei Cinquecento, the busy traffic circle in front of the station. Other European capitals have a monumental central station, but it is immediately apparent that Termini is not exactly a centuries-old museum piece. It is one of the few buildings in the center of Rome that date from the postwar era—the renovation of Mussolini's creation began in 1946, and its festive inauguration took place on December 20, 1950. Since then Termini has been improved and expanded, which has allowed it to become one of the busiest train stations in Europe. In 2006 the station was officially dedicated to Pope John Paul II; later a statue of the pope was unveiled, and it has adorned the Piazza dei Cinquecento ever since.

Stazione Termini was not the first construction on the site. Between 1856 and 1859, the Pontifical States inaugurated the Rome-Frascati and the Rome-Civitavecchia lines, the first two railroads ever built on the spot of the current gigantic station concourse. Rome became a modern city for good when the tiny station built by the pope to accommodate the growing train traffic at the Porta Maggiore was replaced by a fitting concourse. In 1862, the first Stazione Centrale delle Ferrovie Romane opened, but soon thereafter Pope Pius IX commissioned architect Salvatore Bianchi to design a reconstruction project. In 1870, the popes lost their secular power in Rome, which spelled the end of the Pontifical States' political reign. The station's expansions and embellishments were continued under the aegis of the Kingdom of Italy. The station was given a suitable nineteenth-century appearance and from then on was named after the remains of the Baths of Diocletian (*Terme di Diocleziano*) found there. Stazione Termini was born. The large square was named after the five hundred soldiers who died during the Battle of Dogali in 1887, when the Italians suffered defeat in Abyssinia (Ethiopia). Until 1924 the Piazza dei Cinquecento featured a monument for the fallen. It was later moved to a spot in the garden of the Baths of Diocletian.

So one might call the history of Termini and the Piazza dei Cinquecento mostly recent history. Yet it is possible, as soon as we step outside the concourse, to glimpse the earliest history of Rome. When we go out the main exit on the Piazza dei Cinquecento on our right-hand side, we see the remnants of a wall made from enormous stone blocks. A guide would quickly tell you that this used to be the Wall of Servius Tullius, or "Servian Wall," built by the penultimate king of Rome, Servius Tullius. There is little reason to believe that this traditional explanation is true; there is no source from antiquity that supports the idea that Servius Tullius built a wall around the city. We do read, again in Livy, that in the early fourth century BCE the people of Rome started building the city wall (in 378 BCE, to be precise). It is one of the first monumental construction projects in Rome after the fifth century BCE. This period is known among archaeologists as the Crisis Century, culminating in the pillage of Rome by the Gauls in or around 390 BCE, recorded by just about all ancient authors who wrote on Rome.

One could say that, archaeologically, the crisis is reversely traceable; whereas sixth-century BCE Rome still saw the completion of a few public construction projects, and plenty of Attic earthenware and luxury goods still circulated, in the fifth century those signs of prosperity disappeared. The quality of earthenware artifacts declines, and some objects vanish completely, at least from the archaeological records. The written sources usually give a fairly accurate record of what was built and when in Rome, and they remain revealingly silent about the period after 484 BCE (the temples of Jupiter Optimus Maximus, Castor and Pollux, and Saturn had already been built before that year).

At the onset of the fourth century BCE, Rome was, in all likelihood, still a midsized city, but one that was in decline. Ancient and modern historians have possibly exaggerated the impact of the Gauls' pillage, which took place around this time, but it seems clear that the city was struggling to recover from tough times. Our most recent insights connect the pillage to this long period of weakening. The construction of a decent city wall around 378 BCE (as opposed to during the reign of King Servius Tullius) fits well in this historic narrative, especially when we realize that the first neighboring city (Tusculum) had just submitted to Rome.

The Roman Republic had been born, and had stood up and stumbled, but in the early fourth century BCE continued its chosen path filled with optimism and ambition. According to historians, a number of long-lasting historical developments would characterize both internal and external politics in the next two centuries. Inside the city, social relations in particular never ceased to be the topic of debate and the cause of unrest. The patricians, the leading clans that determined everything in politics, society, and economics in Rome, were increasingly bothered by the plebeians, who opposed the patricians' position of power, which they considered to be unjust and excessive. The internal tensions resulted in a fierce class struggle. There were also lingering tensions with foreign peoples in the fourth and third centuries BCE: incessant defense missions and expansion wars set the tone. At first the focus was central Italy, but by 272 BCE, Rome had conquered the entire Italian peninsula, including the Greek colonies in the south. Rome signed treaties with every tribe and city-state it conquered, generally stating that they had become allies of Rome. Although these allies were obligated to supply troops, they were able to maintain a certain degree of autonomy and their own forms of civil rights. Rome also founded colonies everywhere they conquered land, populating them with farmers from Rome or Latium, former soldiers, and Roman citizens who did not own land.

Let's return to Termini, where the remnants of early Rome have now been given some more significance. The "Servian" ramparts of Rome probably enclosed more than one thousand acres, with an estimated population of fifty thousand around the time of its construction. That was just a shadow of what was to come. Around 270 BCE the number of inhabitants had risen to one hundred thousand or even one hundred and fifty thousand, and estimates are that by 200 BCE the city probably housed two hundred thousand people. The steady but massive growth was caused not only by the pull of the big city but also by continued conquests, which led to an enormous number of slaves coming to Rome. Large-scale public waterworks such as the Aqua Appia (312 BCE) and the Aqua Anio Vetus (272 BCE) were the absolute minimum necessary to satisfy the growing need for water in Rome—which, thanks to the city's growing wealth, could be funded too. Together, the two aqueducts carried nearly sixty-six million gallons of water to the city every day.

And this all happened before the great wars of conquest had even begun.

VI

VIA APPIA ANTICA

THE CONQUEST OF THE MEDITERRANEAN

Day in, day out, a constant flow of city traffic and tourists encircle the Colosseum. At the Pantheon they have to join long lines, and the Forum Romanum can also count on a daily influx of visitors. All those monuments are hidden or obscured by buildings constructed in the centuries that followed. In order to get a better look at ancient Rome—with less "noise"—we are going to the Via Appia Antica, one of the city's oldest arterial roads. Along this road the memories of Rome's past emerge every few feet. It is peaceful, and, although the din of the center of Rome is still somewhat audible and occasionally some tourists fly by, we imagine ourselves more in the middle of the countryside with every step we take. With only the green landscape of cypresses and pines in the background, the old steles and tombstones seem to come to life on either side of the uneven boulders, covered with the cart tracks of the Via Appia.

In 312 BCE, an ambitious civil servant, Appius Claudius Caecus ("the blind one"), took the initiative to build this road. He wanted a decent road to the south for the Roman army to travel. This makes sense when we realize that Rome's conquests were becoming increasingly far-reaching; the port cities in the south of Italy were the gateway to the entire Mediterranean. In that year, Appius was censor and in that capacity not only in charge of the census and dividing the population into asset classes but also of the tendering of public works. He built the first aqueduct of Rome (Aqua Appia) and commissioned the construction of a new road to the south, which he named after himself, as he did the aqueduct.

Just about all construction projects in the Republican Period (about 500–30 BCE) were associated with a name (in the case of public works) or an event (most often a military victory, eternalized through a monument or a temple). Today the remains of only a handful of those monuments can be located in Rome, yet it is mostly these types of construction projects that allow us to reconstruct, to a degree, the development of the Early Republic. Similarly, there are only a few contemporary written sources for the Early and Middle Republic (approximately until the first century BCE). The Romans did not begin to record their own history until the second century BCE, and around the same time, Greek authors started to show an interest in the emergence of Rome, which by then was gaining significance as a republic.

What Appius did had become the norm in the late fourth century BCE. As a politician he was a member of the ruling elite, which had totally changed since the founding of the city. The strict distinction between patricians and plebeians had faded due to social shifts: rich plebeians had worked their way up and now belonged, together with the old aristocratic families, to the *nobiles*, the new upper layer of the population that was the main supplier for the Senate. All members of this upper layer belonged to the rank of the *equites* (riders), the highest asset class, since owning a horse had been a distinguishing feature for property since the Regal Period.

In this new social order, assemblies of the people were still held (known as the *concilium plebis* or *comitia tributa* and the *comitia curiata*). Since 494 BCE there had been official advocates of the *plebs*, the plebeian tribunes, who could use their veto power to thwart plans of the ruling elite. The central idea behind the Republic remained unchanged: there was no absolute power, and honor, fame, and influence could only be acquired through actions and deeds during the limited terms you could serve (at least, if you had been born into the right family, of course). Needless to say, it was important for someone like Appius, who was a descendant of the distinguished Claudian family, to work hard at making a name for himself during his administratively active years by serving the "public good" (*res publica*). With construction projects such as the aqueduct and the Via Appia, he did his bit, and he doubtlessly attracted many *clientes*, also judging by his later appointment to consul. But in Roman eyes, real fame could only be acquired in one place: the battlefield—fame that in one case, that of general Scipio Africanus, reached so far that today it is still being memorialized in the Italian national anthem.

The family grave of this hero from the national anthem is located near the very beginning of the Via Appia Antica, on a piece of the road that is now called the Via di Porta San Sebastiano. Two priests, brothers and co-owners of a vineyard on the Via Appia, discovered the entrance to this grave in 1780, by chance, when they were rebuilding their wine cellar. Nowadays you can visit the tomb by appointment, but the space is no longer what it must once have been like: during the centuries before the rediscovery of 1780, tomb raiders had already stopped by. The inscriptions and graves that were identified during the excavations of 1780 were subsequently moved to the Vatican Museums. Nevertheless, the two priests who found the entrance to the burial chambers must have felt quite a bit of excitement when they read "Scipio" in the inscriptions on one of the tombstones. That was, after all, one of the most illustrious families in the history of Rome.

Fratelli d'Italia, l'Italia s'è desta. Dell'elmo di Scipio, s'è cinta la testa—the Italian anthem is a battle song, in which a call is made to lace up one's head in the "helmet of Scipio," the greatest hero of ancient Rome. The Scipioni belonged to the *gens* Cornelia, one of the most prominent families of the Roman Republic, one that could boast a long history of construction projects in the city and that always held important administrative positions. Three male members of the Cornelia family distinguished themselves in extraordinary ways, not in the political arena close to home, but on battlefields far away.

After hegemony had been achieved in Italy, Rome began to look overseas. Its overseas ambitions were not restrained by the fact that the Romans only had an army and no fleet. In 264 BCE, Rome got involved in a conflict on Sicily: former mercenaries from southern Italy had settled in Messina, but they were now under attack from Syracuse. In order to make this threat go away the Messina settlers called on two superpowers for help: Rome and Carthage (North Africa). Carthage enjoyed a solid trading position in the Mediterranean and a strong foothold on Sicily. Rome was the emerging superpower that had made doing business in and around Italy increasingly difficult for the Carthaginians. Both parties feared each other's power, and the matter on Sicily had to end in confrontation. Nobody surmised that the conflict would extend to over one hundred years (off and on) of waging war. Carthage would turn out to be one of the toughest opponents Rome would encounter on the road to world dominance.

The power struggle was initially fought in the so-called First Punic War (264–241 BCE). The word "Punic" is a corruption of "Phoenician," an old name for Carthaginian. Rome won, and Sicily became the first overseas province of the Roman Empire. In contrast to conquered territories on Italy's mainland, which as allies of Rome retained autonomy (and with that a grain of self-respect), these and later provinces immediately came under the authority of a Roman administrator (*praetor*). A few decades of relative peace followed, allowing Carthage to recuperate and conquer territory in Spain. What followed was another confrontation, in what was to become one of the fiercest and most dramatic wars in the history of Rome: the Second Punic War (218–201 BCE). During this war, the Romans met their most formidable opponent of all time: Carthaginian general Hannibal.

The story of Hannibal spoke (and still speaks) to the imagination of friend and foe. Not only did he have the audacity to actively attack the Romans from Spain and to traverse the Alps with a skilled army (including elephants); he was also seen as the mastermind and driving force behind one of the most extraordinary military victories in history: the Battle of Cannae (216 BCE). He crossed the Alps and entered Italy with his troops, wreaking considerable havoc everywhere along the way. Several times there were confrontations with the Roman army. After some modest victories, Hannibal took his troops to Puglia in southern Italy, to retreat for the winter. As a base he chose the small settlement of Cannae, current-day Canne della Battaglia, and he planned on conquering southern Italy. Rome's response was to send the two ruling consuls (Aemilius Paullus and Terentius Varro) to Puglia to lead the army in the battle against the audacious Hannibal.

The nightmare that must have haunted the heretofore always victorious Romans took place at Cannae. The much larger army of Varro and Paullus was massacred: of the 86,000 Romans at least 70,000 were reportedly killed. Hannibal's army of mercenaries was relatively unorganized and exhausted. It was Hannibal's tactical insight that enabled him to crush the well-trained and better equipped Roman army at Cannae. He surprised the enemy by simultaneously attacking them on both flanks and in the rear, encircling the Roman formation. This resulted in the largest military catastrophe that Rome had experienced. It was not until Roman general Publius Cornelius Scipio had gone to Spain and expelled the Carthaginians that the victory of the Romans began to take shape. Eventually, Scipio managed to defeat Hannibal in the Battle of Zama (near Carthage) in 202 BCE, earning him the nickname "Africanus." Carthage surrendered, and Rome could call itself Ruler of the Mediterranean.

Athough Scipio Africanus Maior—the Scipio who is referenced in the Italian national anthem—won the Battle of Zama, many Romans thought that the subsequently signed peace treaty did not do enough to bring the impudent Carthaginians to their knees. "Furthermore, I consider that Carthage must be destroyed," could be heard in the Roman Senate for years. Conservative senator Cato the Elder always concluded his speeches this way, regardless of the issue. During the Third Punic War in 146 BCE, Cato's words became a reality, led by Scipio Africanus Minor (the grandson of the earlier-mentioned Scipio): after the devastating years of war and the Roman victory nearly fifty years earlier, the city in North Africa was completely demolished. All the inhabitants were either killed or sold as slaves. It was an act full of symbolism, not least aimed at Hannibal. The entire Carthaginian territory became the Roman province of Africa.

At the beginning of the third century BCE, Lucius Cornelius Scipio Barbatus, consul in the year 298 BCE and progenitor of the Scipios, built a cenotaph for his illustrious Roman family on the Via Appia. Of course, his own lavishly decorated sarcophagus was given a prominent spot across from the entrance (but is now in the Vatican Museums). The choice for the cenotaph's location, at the beginning of the Via Appia, which had been inaugurated just a few decades earlier, must not have been coincidental. The family (later including Scipio Africanus) was known for being very receptive to cultural influences from the Greeks, and the Via Appia was the main road that had literally paved the way to them, symbolizing the expansion of the Roman Empire toward Magna Graecia, "Great Greece."

Naturally, in spite of Appius's original motives for the construction, the road was not only used by soldiers. Messengers, civil servants, rich citizens, slaves, and all sorts of merchandise traveled the cobblestones of the Via Appia. It was the road leading not only to Sicily and North Africa but also to the trading network of the eastern Mediterranean, from the port city of Brundisium (now Brindisi). The rapid military and economic importance of this route to the south soon earned the Via Appia the nickname *regina viarum*, "queen of the roads."

Nowadays the Via Appia is mostly known from two stories. The oldest story is rooted in early Christian history. A long time ago, the Via Appia was the backdrop of a meeting between Peter and Jesus. Peter had wanted to flee the city via the *regina viarum*, in order to escape the cruel persecution of Christians by the Roman emperor Nero. Once he had reached the Via Appia, he had a vision, in which he met Jesus, who was going in the opposite direction toward the city. Peter asked him: "*Domine, quo vadis?*"—Lord, where are you going? "I am going to Rome, to be crucified again," was the reply. Peter understood the message and did what was expected of him: he turned around and went back to the city to assist the blighted Christian community.

The other famous passage that features the Via Appia as the backdrop is much gorier and more violent. Stanley Kubrick's movie *Spartacus* (1960) tells the story of a slave uprising led by the indefatigable Spartacus, which is eventually crushed by the legions of General Crassus. Around six thousand slaves were captured and one by one nailed to a cross. The wooden crosses were set up by the thousands along the Via Appia, where they would remain for years as a warning.

VII

VIA DI MONTE TESTACCIO

BREAD FOR THE ROMANS

The Roman expansion continued unabated after the outbreak of the First Punic War, not just in Carthage, but in the entire known world. In addition to the provinces of Sicily and Africa, the provinces of Asia (the west coast of Asia Minor), Hispania (Spain and Portugal), and Macedonia (Greece) were among the territories added to the empire. All these conquests initiated an enormous influx, not only of slaves, but also of money and goods, which led to significant changes in the city of Rome. More and more investments were made in what we would now call "urban infrastructure." These investments not only changed the appearance of the city but also provided many jobs. In addition, for the drastically increasing population of Rome the harvest of its own hinterland had not sufficed for awhile: food and all sorts of goods were being imported on a large scale. In the second century BCE, the old harbor at the ford on the Tiber could no longer meet Rome's needs. In its stead a new river port, the Emporium, was built nearby.

From then on, all the goods arriving in the seaport of Ostia would find their way via the Tiber to the new river port and wharf southwest of the Aventine Hill. Thanks to the *Forma Urbis Romae*, the marble city map from the days of emperor Septimius Severus (193–211), which came to us in over a thousand pieces, we know that, around 200 CE, the seaport had been completely built over with so-called *horrea*—warehouses and granaries. Our written sources tell us that the first warehouses were built in the second century BCE. As did other infrastructure construction projects such as aqueducts and roads, *horrea* often carried the name of the magistrate whose idea it had been to raise the funds for them. For example, the Horrea Galbana, of which remains can still be seen, is attributed to Servius Sulpicius Galba, consul in 108 BCE. In 122 BCE, the Horrea Sempronia were built, named after the controversial plebeian tribune Gaius Sempronius Gracchus.

Roman citizens without land or other property found an advocate in Gaius' older brother, Tiberius Sempronius Gracchus, a plebeian tribune from the upper class. For him this was not an ethical issue but more an attempt to solve the army's recruitment problems: only property holders could join the army, so Gracchus ordered state land to be cleared and given to landless proletarians. His plans were met with resistance from many senators; as large landowners they had had personally to invest in state land in many cases, and they did not want to put this arrangement in jeopardy. Tiberius persisted nevertheless and went too far, as he would find out. He tried to push his legal proposal through via the Plebeian Assembly. He wanted the entire project to be financed with Rome's inheritance from Pergamum (the kingdom on the west coast of Asia Minor, bequeathed to the Romans by the last king, Attalus III, and organized as the province of Asia), and he also wanted to run for a second term as plebeian tribune—in the eyes of senators a clear attempt at dictatorship. This was reason enough for the senators to murder Tiberius Gracchus in broad daylight. His land law was found to be an amenable solution for the recruitment problem: it was eventually adopted.

Of the two brothers, the younger, Gaius, was the real rebel; his ideas about redistributing state land and improving the position of the proletarians were even more radical. He managed to retain his position as plebeian tribune for several years, getting one proposal after another adopted by the Plebeian Assembly—to the chagrin of the conservative senators, who feared not only Gaius' political ideals but also, above all, his personal ambitions and his growing support. One of the most famous laws that Gaius Gracchus pushed through was the so-called Grain Law. Thanks to a government subsidy, the price of grain was from then on kept artificially low, at least for Roman citizens. More than ten years after his brother, Gaius was also murdered by nervous senators. His grain law, however, continued its successful run for quite some time.

Following the implementation of the Grain Law, Gaius Gracchus commissioned the construction of "his" Horrea Sempronia in the Emporium, Rome's new port. Roman citizens were now given monthly rations, which meant an abundance of grain had to be produced in the provinces. It was then shipped to Rome, where it was stored in warehouses and could then be sold at a fixed price. It would take another century and a half before the monthly rations of grain were provided to the citizens of Rome for free—the first half of the famous Roman appeasements "bread and circuses."

Nothing is left of Gracchus' granary. The few tangible memories of the Emporium consist of nearly invisible steps and paved slopes, which ran into the water and were intended to facilitate loading and unloading. Even of the Porticus Aemilia, the covered structure directly on the water—with a huge roof supported by close to three hundred pillars—hardly a trace can be found. But it is the Via di Monte Testaccio, the street that shares its name with the entire neighborhood, that takes you back to the times when loads of grain, oil, marble, and other imported goods were unloaded at the foot of the Aventine.

The street winds in a semicircle around the Monte Testaccio. On our way up we walk past the former slaughterhouse (*mattatoio*), where the Roman grain ships must have docked, and where the laborers of the working-class district of Testaccio came to beg for their own rations from 1890 on. To complement their hard-earned wages, they were given the intestines of the slaughtered cattle. This practice laid the groundwork for what we now consider the typical cuisine of this region: classic dishes such as *rigatoni alla pajata* (pasta with calf and lamb organ meat) and *coda alla vaccinara* (oxtail stew) originate from Testaccio. On the other side of the road we see the result of the recently polished image of the old working-class district, also known as "the new Trastevere": the Mercato di Testaccio, built on the remains of the Roman warehouses, part of which is still visible in the middle of the indoor market.

We pause for a moment on the corner of the Via Galbani and the Via Nicola Zabaglia. Although we have already started walking past the artificial mound, here we can see for the first time that this is indeed the Monte Testaccio: the "Mount of Shards," with a circumference of one kilometer and a height of at least 150 feet. *Testa* is Latin for "shard," from which the modern name is derived. The shards come mostly from amphorae and *dolia*, large earthenware pots used to transport great quantities of grain, wine, oil, and other goods from Ostia, via the Tiber, to Rome. From all the conquered territories, goods were shipped to Rome in these pots, and once on land, transported to the *horrea*. Because by law amphorae had to be shattered after usage to avoid possible decay, the dockworkers tossed the barrels onto a large heap, right between the warehouses. Monte Testaccio is actually just a huge Roman landfill.

The "mount of shards" has been researched by archaeologists for a long time. Inscriptions have been found on many shards, often on a piece of a handle or a neck, and all have been neatly catalogued. The shards all date from about the period 150–250 CE, but it is clear that trash was also dumped in the harbor area before that time. Most archaeologists assume that the Monte Testaccio was as tall in the second century as it still is today. The catacombs that have been dug out and now mostly house restaurants and discotheques are recent "additions." It is a strange sensation to be seated in the restaurant Flavio al Velavevodetto and see the shards in the walls. It is a direct reminder of the radically changing world of the ancient Romans, who were no longer the inhabitants of a city but of a metropolis. They no longer lived off their own land but were completely dependent on imported goods to provide for their basic needs. Rome did not have the appearance of a world city yet, but it had in fact become the political, commercial, and social heart of something that was beginning to look more like a global empire.

VIII

PIAZZA DI PORTA MAGGIORE

THE TOMB OF THE ROMAN BAKER

A three-mile walk northeast from the Monte Testaccio into Rome takes you about an hour on modern roads. In antiquity, this would have put you beyond the city walls. Today you might come across the thermae of Caracalla, the ruins of an impressive monumental bathhouse; the overwhelming Colosseum; or the immense Basilica San Giovanni in Laterano. However, none of these monuments had been built at the time of the Roman Republic. Only in the course of the first century BCE did Rome transform itself so that its appearance fit the political and economic status it had acquired on the world stage—though that transformation didn't happen overnight, and the construction of monuments on a large scale didn't appear to be possible until the personal ambitions of successful politicians and generals began to reach great heights.

In contrast, the world of the dead was one in which status, power, and prestige had been carved in stone for centuries. Rome did not allow burials within the city walls—the urban space was considered sacred ground, which could not be fouled by the dead. At the same time, funerary monuments, for those who could afford one, were eminently meant to be seen by others—what good is the memorialization of your life and success if there is nobody to commemorate and admire it? So it would make sense that the wealthier Romans' graves were concentrated right outside the city, on both sides of the roads leading into and out of the city: spots in busy Rome that could count on quite a flow of passersby—on foot, on horseback, or by chariot. You could compare it to billboards, hung in spots that see a lot of traffic every day.

When you take the walk with which we began this chapter, you will find exactly this type of place outside the old city walls. Today it is called the Piazza di Porta Maggiore, after the large city gate that is still standing, and it is as busy an intersection now as it was in ancient Rome. At the time, this was not only the spot where almost all of the city's aqueducts converged but also the intersection of the Via Labicana and the Via Praenestina. Near the gate the remains of those two ancient roads and their courses can still be traced. In 272 CE, the Porta Maggiore itself, formerly the Porta Praenestina or Porta Labicana, was incorporated into the new Aurelian Walls. That was not unusual; along the city limits the many funerary monuments that had lost their meaning and significance were considered an easy way to save time, money, and construction materials. Lying exactly in the path of the wall being built, they weren't demolished but simply included.

The gate, built by Emperor Claudius, is not the oldest monument in this spot, however. Exactly in between the old Via Labicana and the Via Praenestina there is a striking monument, badly damaged on one side, that was erected some eighty years earlier. Even the illiterate Romans (an estimated 85–90 percent of the population) passing this monument must have understood right away what they were looking at: the tomb of a successful baker who had amassed a small fortune from his enterprise over the course of his lifetime. For those who could read, the inscription would tell them the name of the deceased baker: Marcus Vergilius Eurysaces, a Roman baker with a message. How did a Roman citizen see that a baker lay here? The monument could and can be read as a comic strip in stone. For example, at the top (on the frieze) several reliefs feature scenes depicting the daily routines in a bakery (grinding grain, kneading dough, sliding bread into the oven). Workmen (probably slaves) are performing these tasks. They are clearly dressed differently from the robe-wearing characters in subsequent images. The latter are supervising more important matters—the weighing and selling of the bread. The friezes were originally done in color; traces of red and yellow paint have been found. The more abstract, almost fascist-looking decorations on the remainder of the funerary monument, in the shape of round holes and round pillars or tubes, have been (charitably) interpreted as symbolic references to mechanical kneading machines.

Marcus Vergilius Eurysaces lived about halfway through the first century BCE. His nickname, Eurysaces, seems Greek rather than Roman, and nowhere does he indicate whose son he is. Roman citizens typically added their father's name to an inscription (with an "f" for *filius*, "son of," as can be seen on the Pantheon). Historians therefore generally believe that Eurysaces was a freedman—so, a Roman citizen with civil rights, who had a three-part name and who had created considerable wealth for himself, but a former slave nonetheless. This is not absolutely certain: freedmen often specified their social status by adding "lib" or simply "l" to their name: *libertinus*, "freedman."

Whether a freedman or an "ordinary" middle-class citizen, Eurysaces was a rich and proud man. The text on his tomb, across a horizontal strip in the middle, reads:

EST HOC MONIMENTUM MARCEI VERGELEI EURISACIS
PISTORIS, REDEMPTORIS, APPARET

Translation: "This is the tomb of Marcus Vergilius Eurysaces, baker, contractor, he served [. . .]." Opinions are divided about the exact meaning of the last word, *apparet*. The sentence seems to be cut off, which makes interpreting even harder. The funniest theory is that Eurysaces was making a joke: *apparet* would then mean something like "it is obvious" (read: "get it?"). Thanks to the countless references to his profession, it might indeed be quite obvious to everyone that it was a baker who was enjoying his eternal rest. It is not unthinkable that both interpretations of the text are correct and that Eurysaces knowingly included a double entendre in his tombstone text.

From the shipments of grain that arrived from all over the world in the port of the Emporium to the detailed renderings of the grinding of the grain and the baking, weighing, and selling of bread, you can come unbelievably close to the Roman Republic in spots outside the beaten tourist paths. Eurysaces' tomb was discovered by chance in 1837, when Pope Gregory XVI had a tower demolished to "liberate" the Claudian Gate from later additions. The funerary monument of Eurysaces appeared to be hidden in the tower—and, although it would not have been peculiar at all for the Pope to give orders to demolish it, he decided to leave the monument standing in the shadow of the Porta Maggiore. Although the eastern side had been completely destroyed when the grave was incorporated, the tomb was reasonably preserved on three sides. The Pope and fate determined, fortunately, that Eurysaces could stay.

During the excavations, other unearthed objects indicated that there were many more funerary monuments along the two Roman roads. The monument of Eurysaces' wife was also found among the fragments dug up out of the ground. That is, this is what even the most guarded scholars would like to believe. Near the tomb of Eurysaces they found a piece of marble (now in the Museo Nazionale Romano) with the inscription:

FUIT ATISTIA UXOR MIHEI/FEMINA OPITUMA VEIXSIT/ QUOIUS CORPORIS RELIQUIAE/QUOD SUPERANT SUNT IN/ HOC PANARIO

Translation: "Atistia was my spouse/She lived as the most decent woman/her corpse, that which remains of it/lies in this breadbasket." In addition, two marble relief sculptures surfaced, suggesting a husband and wife in typical Roman attire, a couple that without a doubt adorned a funerary monument in Roman times. Whether they represent Eurysaces and Atistia can no longer be determined—let alone whether Atistia was actually really the wife of Eurysaces—but it does create a good story out of all the fragments, perhaps one too good to be true.

IX

PIAZZA DEL TEATRO DI POMPEO

A PROPER THEATER FOR THE CAPITAL

Between the Campo de' Fiori and the Largo di Torre Argentina, right in the heart of the city, hides a small square that takes us to Rome in the Late Republic (first century BCE)—a time of crises and civil wars. Before walking to the Piazza del Teatro di Pompeo, the square that is named after a theater from 55 BCE, we first take a walk across the Via dei Giubbonari and the Via del Biscione. It is hardly noticeable from the ground, but the semicircle that we are making is more or less the same shape as the half-round wall of the Theater of Pompey, the theater that gives the oddly shaped square that lies directly behind the Via del Biscione its name. The current pattern of streets reveals the original location of the first stone theater built in Rome—its remains still concealed in the basements of the (more) modern buildings of this densely populated neighborhood. Part of the original walls and vaults can be seen in some cellars on the Via di Grotta Pinta.

Despite the important role that Rome had begun to play in the political arena following all its conquests, the city itself actually remained quite ordinary and insignificant until about 200 BCE. Certainly compared to the large cities in Greece and Asia Minor, Rome could in no way be called a monumental capital: in the first half of the first century BCE there was no stone amphitheater, no theater, no bathhouse yet. Plays were performed, and gladiator fights were held, but always with temporary stands—wooden scaffolding that could be taken down again. How is it possible that such a great, wealthy, and prominent city, the capital of an empire second to none, still had such an unorganized, chaotic layout?

Farther south, in Pompeii, the locals had watched gladiator fights in a stone amphitheater since 80 BCE. The Romans clearly knew how to build them, but there was no interest.

As true conservatives, senators purposely blocked all plans for such innovations. The republican world, in which power was attainable but always shared and limited to one year, had made absolute power impossible, but at the same time it encouraged rivalry among competitive spirits. Every magistrate and every general was aware that the next commander could easily overturn their successes during a new term. That is why they loved to create permanent reminders in Rome of their triumphs, by financing edifices and erecting victory monuments—preferably bearing their family names. This was exactly the reason the Senate was wary of all monumental public construction projects. A triumphal arch or a victory column was an accepted form of self-aggrandizement, but large public constructions such as theaters or bathhouses, built for the people of Rome in the name of one man, made the senators nervous. That reluctance seems justified, considering the further sociopolitical developments in Rome during the first century BCE.

Historians believe that the short period during which the Gracchus brothers made themselves heard, between 135 and 121 BCE, had a huge impact on the course of history: the ruling elite became internally divided, and violence became increasingly common. A prime illustration is the resulting official separation between the senatorial class and that of the *equites*, or knighthood, in 129 BCE. To make things worse, inside the Senate, opinions were split: although there were still quite a few conservatives, by now called *optimates* ("the best men"), the number of reformists, calling themselves *populares* (derived from *populus*, "people"), was growing. They were politicians in the spirit of the Gracchi, especially in the people's assembly. The differences of opinion between the *optimates* and the *populares* and the fact that the latter group was slowly but surely gaining the upper hand would forever change the course of Roman history.

Someone like Gaius Marius, a competent general (157–86 BCE) who reformed the Roman army, could only have acted the way he did within this new sociopolitical context. He was not old nobility, but a *homo novus*, a "new man" (new money, we would perhaps say today), originally from knighthood. Without invoking an impressive and centuries-old lineage, he got himself appointed consul no fewer than six times. He was behind the Roman legions receiving a standard outfit, he decided that a legion had to consist of fixed numbers (six thousand men and ten cohorts), and he accepted proletarians into the army and equipped them at the expense of the state. In effect, Marius created Rome's first professional army this way.

The increasing state expenses, the commercial needs of the middle class, and the competitive spirit of the elite—all these developments contributed to advances in Rome's imperialism. Conquering new land was the only known means to generate new state income, new commerce, and new honor. Thanks to Marius the number of recruits went up, but historians also detected friction within the ranks of the Roman government. After a certain period of military service, all those proletarian recruits were discharged without any property to fall back on. An army veteran often received substantial payments in money and goods, but what a soldier really wanted after a successful military career was a piece of land to live on. Soon the idea emerged to establish veteran colonies, but even that was met with fierce opposition from the Senate. Just as they were at the time of the Gracchus brothers, senators were wary of the redistribution of land, especially among ex-soldiers. That fear was not unjustified: what would happen if a legion joined forces in a colony and supported its own general?

The senators' nightmares came true: in 88 BCE, following the so-called Social War, during which Italic peoples had risen and provincial elites had acquired a better position, the first Roman civil war erupted. Marius found himself diametrically opposed to another successful commander, Lucius Cornelius Sulla, when both wanted to take charge in the war against Mithridates VI of Pontus (near the Black Sea). The *optimates* supported Sulla, whereas the *populares* wanted to send Marius to Pontus. Sulla took charge and marched with his soldiers to Rome to capture the city—it would have been hard to think of a worse, more brazen act of infamy. He then took his men east, where he won the war against Mithridates. Marius died before Sulla's return. His supporters continued their fight against Sulla's allies, but eventually they had to capitulate. Sulla cleaned house in Rome like no one ever had before: tens of senators and hundreds of knights who had not been on his side were put on the dreaded proscription lists (public sentencing to death) and executed. Sulla tried to secure his position by issuing new laws and reforms. However, he could not establish a new order with lasting success. After his death in 78 BCE, the domestic and external problems in the Roman Empire grew to new heights.

The power vacuum and the political chaos Sulla left behind offered new ambitious men the possibility to rise and attempt to establish order in the Roman Empire. Three men in particular succeeded in pushing to the fore: the extremely rich Marcus Licinius Crassus, the competent Gnaeus Pompeius (Pompey), and a certain *popularis* by the name of Gaius Julius Caesar. At first it was especially Pompey who made a name for himself when he restored order in unruly provinces such as Sicily, North Africa, and Spain. His years of successful fighting in all corners of the Roman Empire had made him a kind of star and given him solid support from loyal legionaries. Naturally, his rising star clashed with that of the other successful general, who was beloved by the "common" people, not only for his conquests but also for his magnanimity: Gaius Julius Caesar. The Senate was less explicit in choosing sides than with Marius and Sulla—the terror and proscriptions were still fresh in the collective memory—and it decided to focus on blocking the plans and dampening the ambitions of all three power-hungry men, Crassus, Pompey, *and* Caesar. The three men responded with a clever move: they joined forces and formed a triumvirate.

While Caesar was organizing expeditions in Gaul and Crassus was sent east to fight the Parthians, Pompey stayed in Rome to restore order there. In 55 BCE, the last stone was laid for the Theater of Pompey, which was named after him. The construction of the theater had not been easy or smooth—senators relied on old laws and blocked construction. The opposition by the obstructionist senators did not deter Pompey. Legend has it that he fooled them by starting construction of a temple for Venus Victrix, the goddess who had led him to his victories, on top of what would later appear to be the bleachers of his theater. He told the grumbling senators that all he wanted was to erect a temple for the goddess. He sold the bleachers as steps leading to the temple. The temple for Venus Victrix did get built, but as an integral part of Rome's very first stone theater complex. Pompey built his theater on the Campus Martius (the Field of Mars), then still a fairly open plain just north of the heart of Rome. The sight of the gigantic, lavishly decorated theater must have made a great impression against the backdrop of that barely developed area of Rome.

The exact location and appearance of the Theater of Pompey are mainly known thanks to a surviving fragment of the Forma Urbis Romae. It was an enormous complex that seated nearly thirty thousand spectators. It consisted of a *cavea*, a semicircular tribune whose shape was copied from Greek theaters and which can still be found in the Via dei Giubbonari and the Via del Biscione; a podium on the straight side of the semicircle; and, behind the podium wall (*scaena*), a large rectangular space with alternating covered colonnades and green trees. The "sacred forest," the name of this green oasis, must have been a nice place to take shelter from the rain or from the bright sun, although loose-lipped gossips claimed it was mainly a secret meeting place for lovers and prostitutes.

Unfortunately, almost nothing of the entire complex of Pompey's theater is visible today, except for the name of the square on the street sign. A small section of the eastern colonnade was excavated on the Largo di Torre Argentina, where the entrance must have been and also the so-called Curia Pompeii, an alternative venue for meetings of the Senate and other assemblies. For example, on March 15 of 44 BCE, the Senate meeting took place here because the Curia on the Forum Romanum had been damaged by fire. That year, the inevitable civil war had already unfolded between Pompey and Caesar after the loss of Crassus, who had succumbed in the fight against the Parthians. Pompeius Magnus, as he had come to be known in the meantime, then died on the shores of Egypt, and so it was Julius Caesar, the last man standing of the triumvirate, who walked toward his violent death on those Ides of March, in the temporary accommodation of the Senate near the entrance of the Theater of Pompey.

The 1748 map of Rome shows that the square now called Piazza del Teatro di Pompeo carried a totally different name in the past: Piazza Pollarola. *Pollame* is Italian for "poultry"; until the fifteenth century little to nothing was known about what was hiding underground, and this was the spot of a special poultry market, which the square was named after. At number 43 we read the inscription CECHOLUS DE PICHIS. Ceccolo Pichi got so rich off this market that he could afford the construction of a beautiful palazzo on the square in 1460. It is a modest form of self-representation in stone, compared to the Roman remains on which the fifteenth-century house was built.

X

PIAZZA DELLA SUBURRA

ROME'S RED LIGHT DISTRICT

Roaming through the ruins of Rome, you may wonder what is left of the common people. In a world where only ten percent were literate, the recorded history—the only source for today's historians—is by definition the history of the elite and only the tip of the iceberg. You can still see remains of that tip everywhere, especially in stone, but can you still find any of the iceberg itself in Rome? We can say with certainty that even the dwellings that have been found, underneath the Palazzo Valentino, for example, belonged to the wealthier, if not the wealthiest, citizens. We are talking about the *atrium* houses also known in Pompeii and Ostia. But in addition to the more luxurious mansions, large "tenement houses" have also been found. These are the types of houses in which poorer citizens lived, like the "apartment building of the Serapis" in Ostia. This sort of living arrangement may sound quite nice, but it was probably far from comfortable: complaints about obnoxious odors and excessive noise abounded, and neighborly quarrels were a regular occurrence.

Did Rome have such apartment buildings too, and if so, where have they gone? According to the poet Martial (second half of the first century CE), it was especially "noisy . . . damp and filthy" in the Subura (derived from *sub urbe*, literally "below the city"; now spelled Suburra), a neighborhood in ancient Rome in which apartment-style dwellings could be found (*Epigrams* 12.18.2, 5.22.5–9). Suetonius (c. 70–135 CE) tells us that Julius Caesar first lived "in an ordinary house" in the Subura—no doubt in the better section of the area—that is, before he became a celebrated general (*Vita Divi Juli* [*Life of Julius Caesar*] 46). He did not move to a new home, his official residence on the Via Sacra, until after his appointment as *pontifex maximus*. More than a century later, Lucius Arruntius Stella, who would become consul in 101 CE, also moved into a house in the Subura, according to Martial. Surely both men didn't live in a tenement house.

The Subura neighborhood in ancient Rome extended from about today's Monti neighborhood to the Esquiline Hill, and it was connected to the Forum Romanum via the Argiletum, an important and busy street. An inscription (SEBURA MAIORE AD NINFAS) was found that suggests the area was divided in two at some point. Subura Maior became the sleazy, noisy part of the area, closest to the Forum Romanum, with all the apartment buildings and shops. Subura Minor, a little higher, was less densely populated and therefore much less dangerous: the buildings were grander and the air healthier. Street names such as Vicus Patricius and Vicus Cyspius indicate that this was where senators and other noble families lived. Martial's consul, who bought a house in this part of Rome in 101, undoubtedly did so in Subura Minor.

High-rise buildings must have been the norm for homes in Subura Maior. Most inhabitants of Rome, generally destitute, lived in *insulae* ("islands"), a name given later to the apartment buildings we know from Ostia, too. The relatively small, dank rooms in such a building, which could have up to five floors, were rented out as apartments. The best apartments were on the top floors; they provided more light and more protection from street noise and stench. However, the top floors were not very safe. Many of these poorly constructed wooden buildings collapsed or burned down. The apartments were not much more than places to sleep: eating, drinking, and personal hygiene were often done elsewhere, at a *thermopolium* (ancient Greco-Roman ready-to-eat places), near fountains, and in public bathrooms. Just like the atrium houses, the Roman apartments faced inward, with a patio in the center. Nobody lived on the ground floor; this was the floor for the stalls of the *tabernae*, the stores that sold goods or services on the street.

Transactions were not limited to goods such as food and delicacies. Martial tells us that the Subura was also a well-known prostitution area, a kind of red-light district in ancient Rome. Walking through the Subura in ancient times must have been a vivacious but dirty, smelly, and dangerous experience. Martial's words breathe a bit of life into the modern marble street sign of the PIAZZA DELLA SUBURRA, on a mostly insignificant and deserted square in the Monti neighborhood.

In addition to the street sign of the Piazza della Suburra, there is also an inscription on the corner of the building right next to the entrance to the subway stop Cavour. The text is part of a commemorative stone that refers to something else that's no longer there: the church San Salvatore alle Tre Immagini. During the papacy of Pope Alexander VI (1492–1503, the infamous Rodrigo Borgia), a certain Stefano Coppo apparently financed the restoration of this church, and it was on that occasion that the following inscription was placed:

ALEXANDRO VI PONT MAX
SUBURA
AEDICULAM SALVATORIS TRIUM IMAGINUM
SUBURANI
AMBITUS REG MONTENTIUM NEMEMORIA
INTERIRET
STEPHANUS COPPUS GEMINIANENSIS S IMPEN IN
CULCTIOREM FORM REDEGIT AEDITUOQ
ANNUOS SUMPTUS
PERPETUO CONSECRAVIT

A loose translation of the last five lines tells us that "Stefano Coppo from San Gimignano has used his own means to embellish the church of San Salvatore alle Tre

Immagini near the Suburra in the neighborhood of Monti, so that it will not be forgotten, and he blessed the church forever by offering annual funding." The church that Stefano Coppo restored was wiped off the map in 1884, due to the unstoppable construction of the arterial road Via Cavour. The inscription was preserved, and it found a spot on the Piazza della Suburra.

XI

PIAZZA SALLUSTIO

CICERO'S AND SALLUST'S ROME

Whereas the area of Subura wasn't a suburb in the modern sense of the word, a kind of *suburbia* did exist on the outskirts of Rome. In the stately neighborhood behind the Via Veneto, terra incognita for most tourists, there is a spot where you can still catch a glimpse of it: the Piazza Sallustio. Caius Sallustius Crispus, Sallust for short, grew up in a relatively well-to-do family in the Abruzzo region. He lived between 86 and 35 BCE, and he was a product of his time: thanks to the Social War, the local Italic elites were taken more seriously, and thanks to a shift in the sociopolitical relationships, there was more room in Rome for "new men." Sallust took full advantage of the new opportunities. He succeeded in working his way up, made a successful career in Rome, positioned himself as diametrically opposed to the *optimates*, and profited immensely from Julius Caesar's successful expeditions. For example, Caesar appointed him governor of Numidia (North Africa). There, Sallust enriched himself greatly, in dubious ways. Exploitation of conquered territories was a typical phenomenon of his time.

Yet Sallust did not enter the history books as a governor or a politician. He is much more well-known as an author and historian, mainly thanks to his book about the war that was fought between 111 and 104 BCE against the Numidian king Jugurtha (*Bellum Iugurthinum*) and his book about the legendary conspiracy of Catilina from 65 to 62 BCE (*De Coniuratione Catilinae*). This does not just make him the most well-known historian from the time of the Roman civil wars; his oeuvre is unique because he wrote about events he himself had lived through.

Lucius Sergius Catilina was a senator on the side of the *optimates* who grew frustrated when his attempts to become consul failed time and again. His family had lost most of its prominence. The old lineage had declined, and, over the years, Catilina had become increasingly poor. Catilina's ire peaked when his third attempt at becoming consul failed in 63 BCE. He noticed that the Senate was becoming increasingly fed up with the triumvirate of Pompey, Crassus, and Caesar, and he saw an opportunity to form a secret coalition (with just about everybody who had some grievance or another) and prepare a coup. He even involved a rebellious group of Gauls in his conspiracy, thus becoming the first true dissident of Rome.

That year Marcus Tullius Cicero was consul, another *homo novus* from knighthood who had worked his way up to the highest political office, in part thanks to his talents as an orator. The four speeches that Cicero dedicated to the conspiracy have gone down in history as classic rhetorical feats. It was Cicero who discovered the conspiracy and disclosed it in the Senate. Pompey's men then rounded up Catilina's gang, and the case was closed. Catilina's conspiracy owes its fame mainly to the surviving works by Cicero and Sallust—in and of itself not a particularly noteworthy incident in Roman history.

Sitting on a bench on the Piazza Sallustio, with not a tourist in sight, you could ask yourself if Sallust had come here just so he could dedicate himself completely to writing historical works. Although the square is now completely developed, in antiquity it was mostly a quiet, green space, far removed from the hectic forum. Underneath our feet are the remains of Sallust's lush private estate on the edge of the city: a villa surrounded by beautiful gardens, a complex called *Horti Sallustiani*. *Horti*, as the Romans called this type of private complex with enormous gardens, had the best of both worlds: they were close enough to the city that one would not miss anything, but far enough away from the city center to escape the worst of the trash and stench.

Sallust must have stockpiled exorbitant amounts of money in Africa. This gave him the means, similar to many other well-to-do Romans in his time, to build a private villa on the edge of the city, surrounded by a green oasis. The gardens were especially impressive: an abundance of plants, trees, and flowers, alternating with a colonnade here and there for a walk in the shade, and fountains or groups of sculptures to daydream by. Everything was interspersed with the most beautiful sculptures, temples, and sometimes even small bathhouses. Sallust's gardens were the largest and prettiest Rome had ever seen.

The remains of the Horti Sallustiani lie in an area where in Sallust's time the city slowly gave way to the undeveloped countryside. When Sallust died, all his possessions, including the *horti*, passed to his son, and after that to his grandson (all named Sallust). These sons, in turn, expanded and embellished the complex. You'd think there would be something left of those illustrious Horti Sallustiani. Archaeological guides of Rome say there is but add that one should not expect too much.

In the middle of the square we go down some stairs. In Rome, going down always seems to be the easiest way to get closer to the past. Once downstairs, we walk into an enormously high space with vaulted ceilings and a few small adjoining rooms. Of the ancient Horti Sallustiani, this is the only structure still standing. Is this all?

A less direct but more impressive way back to Sallust's gardens runs through the museums of Rome. This is where we find the individual sculptures and groups of sculptures that were unearthed in the *horti*. It turns out that some of the most famous sculptures from antiquity once adorned Sallust's green footpaths. The gorgeous *Dying Gaul*, for example, is now one of the masterpieces in the Capitoline Museums, and the *Gaul Committing Suicide* can currently be admired in the Palazzo Altemps. They were probably arranged close together in a place with an artfully imitated historical battlefield. Most of the other sculptures from the *horti*, such as the famous *Ludovisi Throne*, are on display today in the Capitoline Museums or in the Palazzo Altemps. A large number of finds ended up in museums abroad, though.

One object excavated from the Horti Sallustiani is not behind closed museum doors, but on the Piazza Trinità dei Monti: the square you end up on when you scale Rome's most famous stairway, the Spanish Steps. After some detours and wrangling, Pope Clement XII tried to have the obelisk moved to the square in front of the San Giovanni in Laterano. The *obelisco sallustiano*, an enormous obelisk covered in Egyptian hieroglyphs, found a permanent spot here in 1789. Unlike some other hieroglyph-covered obelisks in Rome, the *sallustiano* is not a thousands-of-years-old monument from Egypt. It is, however, an exact replica of such an Egyptian original made during Roman times. The text was copied verbatim from the obelisk that today is on the Piazza del Popolo. By the way, the copyist did make a few mistakes: every once in awhile a hieroglyph is upside down.

Sallust's Rome was more than a city; it had conquered the world and subjected all peoples to it. At the same time, the city that Rome had become in the first century BCE was indebted to those conquered territories in numerous ways. One conquest in particular, which took place around 150 BCE, caused radical long-term changes to the Roman world—and then especially the world of Roman art, culture, architecture, and literature. "*Graecia capta ferum victorem cepit*," the poet Horace aptly wrote (*Epistles* 2.1.156). According to him, uncouth Rome had been "conquered by Greece, which it had conquered." Although the Romans' own creativity and other influences of course cannot be excluded, it is a fact that before the conquest of Greece, there were hardly any sculptures, poetry, prose, or luxury goods in Rome—nor was there a variety of philosophical schools. Contact with Greece breathed life into the intellectual, cultural, and artistic world of an elite that until then had mostly been proud of its old-fashioned frugality and military virtues and had not been too interested in frivolities such as art and poetry. Several high-ranking Greek politicians, authors, and intellectuals ended up in Rome, where they taught prominent Romans not only Greek but also the intricacies of all that Greek civilizations had produced.

Sallust's gardens exemplified the Roman admiration for Greek and Hellenic culture. The breathtaking *Dying Gaul* and *Gaul Committing Suicide* were Roman copies of a Greek original. The practice was so widespread that almost all sculptures we know today from antiquity are Roman reproductions of Greek sculptures. We actually owe our knowledge of Greek sculpture mainly to those Roman imitations. The covered columned galleries or *stoas* that adorned the gardens were structures in Greek style. Some consider Rome's openness to external influence one of the secrets of the empire's success. They made optimal use of their conquests: new peoples were made Roman citizens, consolidating the legions; architectural and cultural practices were copied. The Romans were even open to foreign cults and religions. Inside the already busy pantheon of Roman religion, it was not a problem to add one or two deities. Rome's potential to welcome enthusiastically a "foreign" cult became most apparent when exotic Egypt was added to the empire.

XII

VIA DEL PIÈ DI MARMO

CLEOPATRA, ISIS, AND A MARBLE FOOT

On the Piazza San Marco, the square adjacent to the Piazza Venezia, we meet Madama Lucrezia. She is not exactly beautiful: her appearance is scruffy and tattered. Her worn-down facial expression results in an appearance that can only be called pathetic. The fact that she is tucked away in a corner does not make things better. All in all, it is hard to believe that we are face-to-face with the Egyptian goddess Isis. The name "Madama Lucrezia" was given to the bust in the fifteenth century at the earliest, when Alfonso V of Aragón, King of Naples from 1442 to 1458, presented it to Lucrezia d'Alagno—his mistress. By then, the statue was probably already fairly damaged, but Alfonso V knew that he was giving Lucrezia a special gift: in ancient Rome, the bust of Isis had stood as a cult statue in the large Isis temple, the so-called Iseum Campense. In order to view the second remarkable find in this neighborhood attributed to that temple, we go around the corner, through the Via degli Astalli and the Via di Santo Stefano del Cacco, to the "street of the marble foot," the Via del Piè di Marmo. This marble foot also stood in the *Iseum*, although specialists have determined that the foot is wearing a men's sandal and therefore was not likely part of the same statue as Lucrezia's.

The first time Rome came into contact with Egypt in earnest was during the Second Civil War (49–45 BCE—the first was the one between Marius and Sulla), in which Caesar fought Pompey. When, in the middle of the war, Caesar restored order in Egypt, which Pompey had "pacified" before, there wasn't much left of the great Egyptian Empire of the pharaohs. *That* Egypt had already perished in the fourth century BCE, when Alexander the Great conquered it. After Alexander, Ptolemy I Soter led the country, ushering in a period in which Egypt, as one of the new Hellenistic kingdoms, would be known as the Ptolemaic Kingdom.

Caesar went to Egypt in 48 BCE, where the royal family was entangled in a struggle for the throne. He helped one of the last scions of the Ptolemaic dynasty regain power: the king's daughter Cleopatra VII Philopator. The relationship between Caesar and Cleopatra went beyond what was strictly necessary for politics and diplomacy—this became apparent when nine months later, the Egyptian monarch gave birth to Ptolemy XV, better known as Caesarion. Caesar did not get to enjoy life as a father for very long. After defeating Pompey, he unceremoniously pushed through necessary reforms, thereby acting too much like a monarch and a despot, at least in the eyes of the Senate. These same senators, led by Marcus Junius Brutus and Gaius Cassius Longinus, stabbed Caesar to death on March 15, 44 BCE and left him there, bleeding on the Senate floor.

The discord between *optimates* and *populares* did not go away when Caesar died—and neither did Caesar's supporters. A second triumvirate emerged, consisting of Marc Antony, Marcus Aemilius Lepidus, and Gaius Octavius. One of them, the affluent but for the most part little known Octavius, was only about eighteen at the time. He stated his claim to power when, a few days after Caesar's death, it turned out that he had posthumously been adopted by his great-uncle Caesar as his legitimate son (Caesarion was Caesar's only progeny, but a bastard). Gaius Octavius adopted the name Gaius Julius Caesar Octavianus (more commonly, Octavian); the three men seized power and vowed to avenge the murder of Caesar. And so it came to pass shortly thereafter, in 42 BCE, that the runaways Brutus and Cassius died in the Battle of Philippi. Following that victory, the three men split the administration of the Roman Empire. Lepidus went to Africa, Marc Antony to the east, and Octavian stayed in Italy. Octavian dealt with Sextus Pompeius, the son of Pompey the Great, who seemed to pose a possible threat with his fleet on Sicily. He sidelined Lepidus so that he was in control of the entire west. In the meantime, Marc Antony had also hopelessly fallen for Cleopatra's charms in the east. Together with Cleopatra, Marc Antony behaved a little too much like a Hellenistic monarch, so said the whispers in Rome. Especially in the Senate, they abhorred (stereotypical) oriental despots. To combat this, Octavian pretended to highly value Roman virtues, and ancient ones in particular. It didn't take long for Octavian and Marc Antony to become diametrically opposed to each other. In 31 BCE, Marc Antony and Cleopatra were defeated in the Battle of Actium, leaving Octavian in the same spot in which his adoptive father had been roughly fifteen years before.

The decree to build a large temple for Isis on the Field of Mars in Rome, the Iseum Campense, was issued in the midst of all that hoopla during the second triumvirate in 43 BCE. You would perhaps expect there not to be much room for arts and culture during the long period of civil wars, but the opposite was true. The unrelenting Roman expansion had brought much wealth to Rome. By now, there was great interest in art, culture, and literature in Rome, at least within the upper class—which had been educated "the Greek way" since the second-century BCE conquest of Greece, especially in literature and rhetoric. The Iseum Campense would become the largest and most important Isis shrine in Italy, but construction lasted many decades and was probably not finished until about 40 CE. The location was the Campus Martius (Field of Mars), where Pompey had churned out the first stone theater of Rome about ten years earlier.

Rome's large Isis temple was built right behind the current Basilica di San Marco, after whom Madama Lucrezia's square is named. The temple complex extended out to the Via del Piè di Marmo, the street where the large marble foot from the Isis temple was found. Of course, the temple served for the worship of the cult of Isis (and Sarapis), originally from Egypt. However, it is very possible that a specifically Roman version or interpretation of the cult developed. The Romans were very good at importing and adopting cultural practices from conquered territories. It is not unthinkable that Roman legionaries, who sometimes spent years in a far corner of the empire, simply embraced certain customs by themselves. In the case of Egypt, it was not only the Isis cult that was exported; in Sallust's gardens and at other excavations, countless art objects that were imported from Egypt or allude to Egyptian (high) culture were found. In a world in which sculpture, relief, and architecture were the only media to communicate a message to a large audience and in which the wealth of the competitive elite kept growing, conspicuous consumption was to be expected.

The Isis that the Romans came upon in the land of the Nile had long ceased to be the old Egyptian deity from the time of the pharaohs. It had been hellenized since Alexander the Great's conquest of Egypt and the subsequent period of the Ptolemaic Dynasty. Today it may be difficult to imagine how a deity and even an entire cult could adapt like a chameleon to local traditions and cultures—the currently reigning monotheistic religions often claim to hold the only correct interpretation of the book through which they justify their belief system. But if you were to study Catholicism—a faith spread around the entire world yet grounded in one idea and one basic book—more closely at local levels in modern Africa, Asia, and South America, you would find that Catholicism, most certainly in the beginning, was adapted to or at least fit into older traditions and local customs where possible. We should therefore not be surprised that when we meet Madama Lucrezia, who is actually Isis, she does not look at all like the standard pictures of Egyptian goddesses we have in our heads. "A Roman version of a foreign deity" would be a more apt description. Archaeologists recognized and interpreted the statue as the Egyptian goddess based on her hairdo and clothing, but except for the so-called "Isis button" between her breasts, these characteristics can even be called downright Roman.

In yet another, chronologically later respect, Madama Lucrezia is truly Roman. Together with five other statues in Rome, she belongs to an illustrious group of critical minds with razor-sharp tongues: the so-called Congress of the Wits (in Italian: *Congresso degli Arguti*). The six of them are also known as "the Talking Statues of Rome," revealing a Roman tradition originating in the fifteenth century. Concerned citizens wrote critical messages on small pieces of paper, often addressed to the reigning Pope, and they stuck these onto one of the six statues, enabling these six statues to speak for them and for all of Rome. As the only female among the talkative male statues, Madama Lucrezia has always been the quietest. She can almost size up one of her more famous (and much less decrepit) fellow statues, the once quite garrulous Marforio. From her forgotten corner on the Piazza San Marco, she has overlooked the Capitoline Museums for centuries, whereas he was given a prominent spot in the Palazzo Nuovo.

XIII

PIAZZA AUGUSTO IMPERATORE (I)

THE UGLIEST SQUARE IN ROME

The entire city carries traces of Augustus. At the Forum of Augustus we witness the commemoration of his victory at Philippi: the remains of the temple of Mars Ultor, "the avenger," erected as a monument for the day of reckoning for Brutus and Cassius, the killers of Caesar. On the other side of the Capitoline, in what would later become Rome's Jewish ghetto, a small part of the theater of Marcellus remains on a street by the same name. It used to seat about fourteen thousand spectators. Caesar started construction, but it was Augustus who finished and inaugurated the theater around 13 BCE, dedicating it to his sister Octavia's son, Marcellus. Immediately adjacent to the theater was the temple of Apollo, rebuilt (entirely in marble) by Gaius Sosius, ex-consul from Augustus' inner circle. This is the temple of Apollo Sosianus, of which today exactly three columns remain. Apollo's temple, in its turn, was flanked by the Porticus Octaviae, which Augustus built around the temples of Jupiter Stator and Juno Regina, in honor of his sister, and of which the entrance gate is still there (and the street name, Via del Portico d'Ottavia). On Rome's streets and in its museums, one can find countless other monuments, obelisks, sculptures, and inscriptions that together bring the Augustan Age to life. However, nowhere in Rome is Augustus as palpable as near the monuments on the Piazza Augusto Imperatore, considered by most to be one of the ugliest squares in the historic center of Rome.

Augusto Imperatore, or Emperor Augustus, was still simply Gaius Julius Caesar Octavianus when he defeated

Marc Antony in the Battle of Actium in 31 BCE. Having eliminated his last opponents, Octavian found himself basically at the same crossroads as Caesar after the death of Pompey: as the only one of a triumvirate remaining. However, the road Octavian decided to take at this point was different from that of his adoptive father. At the end of his road, Caesar found the *optimates*, who were ready to stab him to death with the knives they had kept hidden under their togas, in a bloody conspiracy to save the Republic from destruction in the nick of time. At the end of the road that Octavian had chosen, those same conservative senators were ready with a unique and exceptional present: the honorary title of Augustus, which roughly translates as "the exalted." He had taken a (symbolic) step backward, and for that very reason he was encouraged to take an extra step forward. How did Octavian, still only in his mid-thirties, accomplish that? Why do we call Augustus "the first emperor of Rome," and how does one begin an empire?

"After ending the civil wars and having obtained the highest power by universal consent, in my sixth and seventh consulates, I passed the state from my power into the hands of the Senate and the people of Rome. In gratitude for this deed, by Senate decree, was bestowed on me the title of 'Augustus.'" These are Augustus' own words, engraved on the sidewall of the Museo dell'Ara Pacis, the modern lodging of the Ara Pacis Augustea, west of the Piazza Augusto Imperatore. So, according to that thirty-fourth paragraph of his public testament, known as the *Res Gestae Divi Augusti*, which was published and spread throughout the empire following Augustus' death, he handed power back to the Senate and the people of Rome (the famous republican phrase *senatus populusque romanus*, SPQR). He put an end to the civil wars and restored the Republic, and as a reward, the most traditional republican body offered him the monarchy on a silver platter.

Exactly how and why we will probably never know, but the two events were closely linked to each other. During a series of Senate sessions in 27 BCE, the state of emergency caused by the civil wars officially ended. At these sessions it was also decided that Augustus should give up the far-reaching legal authority temporarily conferred to him to restore order. He could have abused his exceptional constitutional position, but he decided to hand back all his special powers to the Senate voluntarily, respectfully, and humbly instead. The senators were very well aware that this could have ended differently; in 43 BCE, they had met with Augustus' cruel side when (together with Marc Antony and Lepidus) he eliminated his political enemies with the merciless proscription lists. They expressed their gratitude by bestowing the honorific "Augustus" on Octavian. Using his diplomatic talents, Augustus, the posthumously adopted son of Caesar, achieved something Caesar himself was too impatient and perhaps too much of a bully for. It is one reason that *festina lente*, "hurry slowly," is known in history as one of Augustus' guiding principles. Go straight for your goal, but proceed with caution.

No matter how noble Augustus' objectives were in his own mind, in the middle of the Piazza Augusto Imperatore we see the stone symbol of the intentions and ambitions that Augustus cherished from the beginning: a monumental tomb for himself and his family. It was in 32 BCE already—before Augustus had won his struggle with Marc Antony in Actium—that he gave the green light for the construction of this mausoleum, which was seemingly inspired both by Etruscan tombs and the famous primordial mausoleum in Halicarnassus. The Ara Pacis monument in the museum is no longer in its original spot, but the mausoleum has always been there. It fell into oblivion, was reused for all sorts of other purposes, and suffered from neglect. It is still there, exactly where Augustus built it more than twenty centuries ago. At the time that was a logical place for a tomb: along the Via Flaminia, which ran north from the gate in the "Servian" wall along the Field of Mars. That is now the Via del Corso, which is separated from the Piazza Augusto Imperatore by the seventeenth-century San Carlo al Corso and the *palazzi* from the fascist period. Once finished, the mausoleum did not stand alone. The entire current Piazza Augusto Imperatore and the surrounding area were eventually included in Augustus' large-scale building plans.

Octavian accepted the honorific "Augustus," but he let the Senate keep its traditional institutions, its *cursus honorum*—and with that, its dignity. He ensured himself of absolute power, slowly but surely, by subtly bending all laws of the Republic to his will, leaving only the facade of the Republic intact. It was perhaps an empty shell, but one that saved conservative senators from losing face. The Senate and the people of Rome accepted the new situation, not least because finally an end had come to nearly one hundred years of civil wars and bloodshed—a Roman citizen born in the forties BCE had almost never known peace; neither had his father or grandfather. It was no coincidence that *pax*, peace, became one of the priorities of Augustus' PR machine.

Internal peace, a Rome free of civil wars, was only the beginning. After 27 BCE it became Augustus' mission to pacify the borders of the empire and to suppress insurrections by rebellious tribes. His honorific was accompanied by the supreme authority (*imperium proconsulare*) over the provinces with the most troops (Gaul, Spain, and Syria). Although Augustus was not much of a military man himself, his friend and confidant Agrippa was a skilled general who would achieve many victories under the emperor's banner, as would the sons of Livia, Augustus' second wife. As a sidenote, Augustus himself preferred not to use titles such as "emperor," but "Caesar" (Latin pronunciation "kaí-sar") was part of Augustus' official name and as such it was adopted in modern European languages as synonymous with autocrat ("Keizer" in Dutch, but also, for example, "Czar" in Russian). Because, on paper, Augustus had left the Republic intact, he did not immediately choose a title that suggested a new type of kingship. Historians talk about "the principate" of Augustus, after the title *princeps*, which was used often, but not officially: "first among equals." Other honorifics would follow, such as *pater patriae* ("Father of the Nation"), but Augustus only became emperor retroactively, when the first historians claimed the Roman Empire started with him.

Augustus remained cautious. Between 27 and 23 BCE, the regulation of electing a new consul every year was still in effect, but in 19 BCE, the consular powers were permanently conferred to him. His power base was solidified even more when he was given the *Tribunicia Potestas* ("Tribunician Power") for life. Since Augustus had come of age in the era of civil wars, he knew that there would always be enough political foes and that his position was precarious, for now. There was a need for peace but also for order. Augustus would need a holistic view and capital if he wanted to keep everybody happy and look forward to a long and stable reign. He needed to run a smooth administration and tax collection, a sound organization of civil servants and secretarial services—which he personally supervised both for Rome and for the provinces of the empire. In response to any personal request, imperial decrees had to be issued and accorded legal standing, so that Augustus could become the ultimate *patronus* of all Romans, his clients. Because Augustus had been carrying out the tasks of the censor since 28 BCE, he was the designated person to implement formally all the necessary reforms. By effecting changes in all aspects of Roman society (as well as in the Senate, the army, and the grain and water supply in Rome), Augustus made sure that anyone who was important or who could, dissatisfied, try to grab power—from senators to knights to soldiers—was linked to him. He ensured they had chances to work their way up the socioeconomic ladder and would benefit from the peace he had brought to the empire.

The peace stabilized (and enlarged) the emperor's revenue stream, which provided him the means to finance his construction and restoration projects in the capital, enabling architecture and art (for propaganda) in general to flourish. Augustus considered visual imagery to be one of the most important means through which he could give his government a symbolic thrust. A variety of art forms were employed for his propaganda, combined with an extensive building program. The media that were at his disposal for relaying his message were mainly visual arts, inscriptions, and imagery on coins. Over a century later, biographer Suetonius summarized Augustus' administration in one now famous sentence (which should be taken metaphorically rather than literally): Augustus found a city of bricks but left behind one of marble.

Of course, the common thread in all the visual imagery was always *pax*. Augustus decided to celebrate peace by erecting a monumental "peace altar"; the Ara Pacis, now housed in a super-modern museum, on whose wall we can read Augustus' testament. Originally, the altar had little to do with the *Res Gestae* inscriptions—those were placed on both sides of the entrance to Augustus' tomb in accordance with his wishes, and copies were disseminated throughout the empire. The Ara Pacis was consecrated in 9 BCE. The building was to be a masterpiece of Roman relief sculpture, and a symbolic ode to the peace and prosperity that Augustus had brought to Rome. That message was communicated in a language that almost everybody could understand: beautiful symbolic and mythological reliefs adorned all sides of the altar. The Ara Pacis, pieces of which were found on the Field of Mars, joined the earlier mentioned mausoleum and an Egyptian obelisk that once belonged to pharaoh Psamtik II, which Augustus brought from Heliopolis to Rome to be erected on the Field of Mars. For a long time it was assumed that this obelisk served as a sundial, but that theory has been increasingly questioned in recent years. It is more likely that the obelisk was a monument for the victory over Egypt. That takes nothing away from this obelisk, which we pass on our way to the Piazza Augusto Imperatore (on the Piazza di

Montecitorio) and the entirety of the special monuments that Augustus collected in this bend of the Tiber.

In antiquity, some problems arose on the Field of Mars due to ground elevations, probably caused by the many times the Tiber burst its banks. People tried to protect the monuments to no avail. The Ara Pacis disappeared underground for seventeen hundred years and was forgotten. The memories of Augustus' "golden age" never died, though. Until his death in 14 CE, he ruled the Roman Empire and the city he made "of marble"—an impressive reign that lasted more than forty years. In fact, his principate meant the end of the Roman Republic, which had lasted for almost five hundred years. And to think that the Romans swore, when their last king was expelled, that they would never again let one person have all the power.

On the sun-warmed, white steps of the Ara Pacis museum, a question arises that not only historians but many others have posed since antiquity. How can we explain Augustus' unprecedented success? Most of his legal powers had also been in the hands of other skilled generals and aspiring absolute rulers. Patience and caution, however, made Augustus a fundamentally different figure than the pretenders to the throne who preceded him. The countless reforms Augustus implemented show not only his political genius but also an impeccable feel for diplomacy and an eye for long-term planning. Face-to-face with his Ara Pacis and eternal resting place, we can easily imagine that Augustus, more than anyone else, understood that at the height of the Roman Empire, to a certain extent, it did not matter much what actions you did or did not take; much more important was the way in which you packaged everything, the *story* you created and communicated around those actions. The scale and systematic manner in which that happened under Augustus had no precedent.

The story of Augustus—the birth of a Roman Golden Age of peace, success, and affluence, in which the norms and values of the forefathers, the virtuous founders of the global empire, would come to life again under a leader who wanted to be a father rather than a monarch for his people—was told in every way possible and with all the media available in an ancient city. The use of a legendary heroic past for the entire people, in the style of the Greeks, which gave meaning to present-day Rome, can be called a small stroke of genius. That was the kind of story that every right-minded Roman—even the literati, who must have figured out something was going on that they principally opposed—was receptive to, a story that they must have told with pride. To put it in modern terms, it was an enormous marketing success.

XIV

VIA MECENATE

THE LITERARY CIRCLE OF MAECENAS

After having walked on and around the Capitoline and Aventine Hills and the area of the former Field of Mars, it is time for us to go to a different part of the city that still bears traces of ancient Rome, the Esquiline Hill. After all, it is one of the seven hills on which the city was founded; it is also where some of the oldest objects from ancient Rome were dug up. The modern neighborhood Esquilino does not entirely line up with the hill: it only covers the area southeast of the Via Merulana. The Monti neighborhood and the Colle Oppio, to the northeast, are both located on the Esquiline Hill. From metro stop Vittorio Emanuele, we walk down the Via Leopardi, in the direction of the Colle Oppio, to reach the Via Mecenate.

This is Rome during the Imperial Period. That is, this *was* it, beginning in the first and second centuries CE, when buildings such as the Domus Aurea, the Colosseum, the Baths of Titus, and the Baths of Trajan arose. These were gigantic constructions, projects so enormous that they were really only possible within the context of a monarchic system. Augustus laid the solid foundation for this system. Under that same Emperor Augustus, it was still relatively quiet on this hill. There were only private homes with scattered shrines in between. The old city stopped here too. The city wall ran somewhere between the Piazza Vittorio Emanuele and the Colle Oppio. It was the kind of neighborhood that was perfect for building nice private villas surrounded by ornamental gardens—like the nearby Horti Sallustiani. A certain Gaius Cilnius Maecenas, a descendant of a wealthy family of Etruscan origin, owned such a villa here. Unfortunately, the Via Mecenate, named after his *horti*, no longer discloses what is hidden underneath it. If you want to get closer to the past, it would be better to find a spot among the ruins of the Parco del Colle Oppio.

Maecenas often represented Augustus on trips abroad. Even though the state government Augustus reformed required him to make those trips, the emperor could not possibly do so personally. He had representatives go in his stead, and Maecenas slowly became Secretary of State *avant la lettre* for the Augustan government. But he was more than that. Thanks to his diplomatic talents he worked his way up to personal adviser, confidant, and friend of the emperor. Because Maecenas was an art lover through and through, and the emperor and his close friends loved to surround themselves with the best poets, speakers, and authors, he also made sure the government supported a number of authors and poets. In this way the Augustan government quite literally sponsored the heyday of Latin literature.

Before his political career took flight, Maecenas had spent his inherited wealth on his hobby: poetry and literature. On the Esquiline he built a large villa with beautiful ornamental gardens. These Horti Maecenatis gained fame as the spot where Maecenas brought together the best poets of his time. Among them were outstanding poets like Virgil, Propertius, Horace, and Ovid. Maecenas created a literary circle, brought its members together frequently, and made his own home its center. And don't think that they limited themselves to pompous poetry readings; Maecenas' exuberant parties on the Esquiline were at least as legendary.

Politics and art met not only figuratively through Maecenas but also literally: as a close friend of Augustus, Maecenas ensured that the literary talents of men such as Virgil and Horace were employed in the emperor's "propaganda machine." The poets and novelists were often financially dependent on the Maecenas-Augustus duo, and they created some of the greatest literary masterpieces of antiquity. Maecenas went down in history as the first great sponsor and *patronus* of the arts. That is why his name lives on in almost all languages: in the course of the centuries, "mecenas" has become synonymous for "patron and benefactor of arts and culture."

During this heyday of Latin literature, an ambitious man from the countryside named Livy made a name for himself as chronicler of the Roman Republic. He did not belong to Maecenas' or the emperor's circle, but he did write down the history of Rome, from the foundation of the city until his time. It was high time, he said, that this was done: "If any people should be allowed to lend its origin a certain sanctity by referring it to a divine will, it would be the Roman people: so great is Rome's military glory that when it calls none other than Mars its father and the father of its founder, all of Earth's peoples will accept this with the same resignation as they accept Rome's authority."[1] It is mainly through Livy that we also know the famous founding myth of Rome. The story of Romulus and Remus was not recorded until the second century BCE, and there were several versions going around. It is primarily Livy's version that is now known all over the world, two thousand years later.

It is not happenstance that a certain Virgil, indirectly commissioned by Augustus himself, was working on the first truly Roman epic between 30 and 19 BCE. Virgil, forty years old when he started this work, had taken on an honorable but complex task that others had declined. He was to write an epic about the Roman people, a unifying story that would affirm the oneness of Rome, now that the contentious era of civil wars was over. At the same time, he had to make sure his most important client would not be poorly served. Making Augustus himself the main character would evoke too many associations with the adoration of rulers in Rome. And thus

[1] Livy, *Rise of Rome* (trans. Luce).

Virgil wrote an epic about the adventures and wanderings of a Trojan prince, who fled his hometown during the Trojan War (known from the Greek epic tradition) and, encouraged by a prophecy, went to look for a new country to be founded. The name of this hero, who would become the legendary primordial Roman, was Aeneas. Via his illustrious adoptive father, Gaius Julius Caesar, Augustus claimed to be a descendant of Aeneas, as was depicted on the Ara Pacis. Of course, this saddled the main character of Virgil's *Aeneid* with a double role: he was the pater familias of Augustus and his family but also the progenitor of the Roman people. The reign of Augustus, the peaceful and prosperous times for Rome—thanks to Virgil's masterpiece—seemed to have been written in the stars.

Walking through the Parco del Colle Oppio, you will find it difficult to imagine what a typical evening with literary guests, wine, and improvised poetry in Maecenas' home must have looked like. Little remains of the Horti Maecenatis, despite the once infamously lavish complex, and especially of the ostentatious gardens—they reportedly added a vineyard and a swimming pool filled with hot, thermal water. We do know, however, where they were located: Maecenas' villa was built on the Esquiline between 42 and 35 BCE, in the area around the current-day Via Mecenate ("Mecenate" is the Italian name for "Maecenas"). The so-called Auditorium of Maecenas, found during excavations in the nineteenth century, is all that remains (it can be seen near the Largo Leopardi)—that is, if the interpretation of the underground space is correct. It is a large hall with an apse and several structures for the water supply. It may not have served as an "auditorium" but as a dining hall (*triclinium*).

The many finds made in this area attest to the fact that Maecenas' gardens were filled with luxury and splendor. Many of these finds can be viewed today in the Capitoline Museums. The Museums feature an entire hall dedicated to the Horti Maecenatis (the *Sala degli Orti di Mecenate*), which is worth a visit. Walking among the Museum's mosaics, sculptures, and other pieces of art that once adorned the complex will give you a better impression of Maecenas' city villa than will the Via Mecenate.

XV

VIA DELLA VII COORTE

"I AM TIRED; BRING IN MY REPLACEMENT"

Trastevere is the neighborhood across the Tiber where tourists stay primarily to enjoy Rome's nightlife. Its status as an entertainment area is well deserved, although the influx of tourists has resulted in a significant decrease in authentic Italian establishments. At the same time, Trastevere has a reputation of being a prime example of Rome's "working class neighborhoods." What all those tourists in Trastevere do not know is that the local police headquarters of the ancient Trans Tiberim lie hidden underneath this labyrinth of alleys. Traces of emperors and rich people are abundant in Rome, but you would not expect a group of ordinary cops to be of much archaeological interest. Even more amazing is that you can catch a glimpse of these police officers in the modern street name index. Reason enough to cross the Tiber via the Ponte Garibaldi, at Tiber Island, and look for the "street of the seventh cohort."

The seventh cohort, or Cohort VII, was the brigade in charge of ensuring public order. You could call them Roman community police. The Via della VII Coorte is named after that brigade, and not without reason (does anything happen without reason in Rome?). Hidden behind the doors of house number 9, we find the entrance to the Excubitorium dei Vigili. *Excubitorium* is likely derived from the Latin *ex cubare*, "to lie outside." In other words: keeping watch. Several sources from antiquity tell us that Cohort VII was established around the beginning of the Common Era and that the brigade was tasked with guaranteeing fire safety in the neighborhood. The Excubitorium, discovered by archaeologists in the Via della VII Coorte in the nineteenth century, could not be dated earlier than the second century CE. Where the brigade was housed before that time is uncertain. The discovery of the remains was actually coincidental, as is often the case in Rome: workers stumbled upon them during building restorations in the area.

Although initially the archaeologists were enthusiastic—the first ones on the site found some Roman graffiti on the walls—the place was abandoned fairly quickly and literally left to its own fate. The years, the humidity, and the neglect did not improve the condition of this Roman dig. One hundred years passed before it was decided that this site of an ancient Roman fire brigade had enough historical value; authorities temporarily shut it down and began restoration. In the meantime, the graffiti on the walls had become illegible and in some cases had completely disappeared. The archaeological work done between 1966 and 1986, however, did yield much new information. The Excubitorium turned out to date back to the Imperial Period. Initially it was probably used as a private dwelling, but toward the end of the second century it was turned into a "fire station" of the seventh cohort, also known as Cohortes Vigilum.

The brigade, covering the ancient Roman areas of Trans Tiberim (neighborhood XIV) and Circus Flaminius (neighborhood IX), was established by Emperor Augustus in 6 CE. The cohort had seven thousand men and was led by a city prefect. The seventh cohort's task of keeping the neighborhoods safe was 24/7. In ancient Rome this normally meant responding to fire, but also included riots or other public disturbances. *Ubi dolor ibi Vigiles* was their proud motto: "Where there is pain, we are its fighters." The former fire station of Cohort VII is now about twenty-five feet below current street level. There is a large hallway that once featured a mosaic floor symbolically indicating the most important task of the cohort: putting out fires. There are several rooms with decorations such as pilasters with Corinthian crowns and some frescoes. Judging by the graffiti that was there earlier, the leader of the brigade likely used a separate room. There is more certainty concerning the identification of other rooms: some "barracks" have been found, but also a toilet area and a stockroom for grain, oil, and other foodstuffs.

Because much of the graffiti the Roman firefighters left behind on the walls of the Excubitorium deals primarily with life in the fire station, the graffiti is actually the most suggestive remains. The messages are very hard to read, but much was documented when they were first discovered. The brigadiers wrote these messages on the walls between 215 and 245 CE, always in a moment of rest or "break"—when they were not keeping watch in the neighborhood. In some cases, they thank the emperor or gods for something, and sometimes the texts talk about the *sebacaria*. This word is not known from other contexts, so the interpretation is somewhat uncertain, but it seems to be about a certain shift that lasted a full month. The shift was not without risk: the message *omnia tuta* ("all's well") was found more than once on the walls. The shift was also tiresome, demanding much from the men. One of them wrote on the wall: *Lassus sum successorem date*—"I am tired; bring in my replacement."

XVI

VIALE DELLA DOMUS AUREA

THE PALACE BURIED BENEATH THE COLOSSEUM

In antiquity, the wildest stories about the palace of Emperor Nero made the rounds. Its nickname was the "Golden House," and it must have been one of the most megalomaniacal construction projects Rome had seen by then. First, it was enormous. Suetonius, the first/second-century CE Roman biographer of the emperors, wrote: "Its vestibule was large enough to contain a colossal statue of the emperor a hundred and twenty feet high; and it was so extensive that it had a triple colonnade a mile long. There was a pond too, like a sea, surrounded by buildings to represent cities."[1] The hallways and rooms housed so many paintings and rich decorations that the Romans soon enough called it a golden house (*domus aurea*). Nero's new dwelling also featured many technological gadgets. Reportedly, the ceilings of the dining rooms continuously spun around, while flower petals and sweet-smelling perfumes came down on the guests in a salutary mist. In the entrance hall of the palace, the enormous statue of Nero, nicknamed the *colossus neronis*, symbolized his infamous megalomania.

The leaders of Rome after Caesar and Augustus were less successful at inspiring the interest of the public at large. The first emperor's PR was so effective that he has been in the spotlight for more than two thousand years. Augustus' family (in-laws) remained in power for another half century and supplied four emperors during that time, but they

[1] Suetonius, *The Lives of the Caesars*, trans. J. C. Rolfe, 2 vols., Loeb Classical Library (Cambridge, Mass., 1950), vol. 2, section 6.31.

are most often referred to, in short and collectively, as the "Julio-Claudian dynasty." If anything is known about these emperors individually, it is their weird traits (Caligula the sex debauchee who made his horse consul; Claudius the stutterer, mostly known thanks to *I, Claudius*). Nero's place in history is as perhaps the blackest of black sheep. It's not clear whether the image of Nero as narrated by the writing elite of Rome (senators who did not like him) closely matches reality. The slander was effective, that's for sure; Nero's despotic behavior had become legendary by the Middle Ages. In any case, he was the closing entry of his dynasty: Nero had not chosen a successor, giving the stage to a new *gens*. After a brief period of chaos, the Flavians established their dynasty in Rome.

There is no doubt Augustus had a substantial impact on Rome's construction and restoration policies. However, you only need to look at the Colosseum, knowing that that enormous amphitheater was not yet there when Augustus died in 14 CE (and that a gigantic palace had to be razed before it could be built), to realize that early Imperial Period Rome was not only Augustus' city. The cityscape would change drastically through the many building projects, which around the time of the "invention" of the *principate* by Augustus were able to get off the ground more easily. People often picture ancient, imperial Rome as some sort of well-designed ensemble of colonnades and impressive marble buildings. When we understand what lies beneath the Viale della Domus Aurea, the extension of the Via Mecenate, we can also easily imagine that living in Rome in the first century CE may have been much like living on a permanent construction site. That was surely the case when Nero decided that he needed a new palace.

The rulers of the empire had resided on the Palatine since Augustus, who was born there. Nero, who became emperor in 54 CE, also had his palace there. He was busy greatly expanding it toward the Esquiline when a large fire erupted in 64 CE. According to ancient sources, the devastating flames incinerated almost two-thirds of the city—including the imperial palace. Nero seized the opportunity: now he could finally build a dignified palace for himself. Scandal-mongers, who enjoyed gossiping about Nero anyway, claimed that he himself had started the fire. Anyhow, the smoke had barely dissipated when the grounds were designated for the construction of Nero's Domus Aurea. But where did Nero's palace end up? The answer to that question, as with so many places, can be found in the catacombs of the current city. The street name sign marking VIALE DELLA DOMUS AUREA and the Colosseum are the only above-ground indications that point to the location of the palace, a tiny bit of which has been excavated. The Flavians, who came to power after Nero, cast an effective *damnatio memoriae* over Nero and his administration: all reminders of him had quite literally to be erased. Perhaps the stories about the Domus Aurea in the literature are exaggerated and there was simply never much outrageous stuff to be found. Or maybe that *damnatio memoriae* was just incredibly effective. In any case, it would take no less than fifteen hundred years before reminders of Nero's Domus Aurea would come to light.

On January 14, 1506, Felice de Fredis happened to be digging on his estate in Rome. He was working in the dirt with his hoe—and in the Eternal City that always yields something. De Fredis hit a hard stone underground. He had no idea that his find would forever change Western European (art) history. The man was apparently standing on top of one of the vaults of the Domus Aurea, the long-lost golden palace of Nero. At that time, an art-loving pope, Julius II, reigned in Vatican City, and he immediately sent a delegation to examine the find more closely. Michelangelo was among a group of artists and experts who reportedly descended into the dark, hollow spaces. What their eyes witnessed there enraptured them: rooms adorned with frescoes, marble ornaments, and sculptures. For centuries, nobody had set foot in these spaces, and now they were the first ones to see them again. The find would have a profound impact on late Renaissance painting. After the Renaissance artists visited the underground Domus Aurea, a new art movement emerged—"grotesque"—named after the "grottoes." This movement accounted for the abundance of painted ornaments discovered from this period.

If you put on the required miner's helmet and wander through the underground tunnels of the palace nowadays, it is quite difficult to have the same experience as Michelangelo. The frescoes, which he must have seen in lively colors despite the darkness, have lost their color, shine, and clarity over the course of the centuries. The historically sensational idea that Nero may have walked these corridors can grab ahold of you every now and then, but it is kept in check by the knowledge that we should distrust any "certain" archaeological identification of ruins with a famous building from the Roman sources. British classicist Mary Beard described this once as the "terrible temptation to equate what we can see with what the Romans have written about." She surmises that the excavated part of the Domus Aurea surrounding the space identified as the "turning dining hall" (which we know through Suetonius) could actually very well be the slave quarters of the palace, but I digress.

Destroying the reminders of Nero, the last descendant of the Julio-Claudian dynasty, was not enough for the new imperial family. The Flavians were newcomers who still needed to win the favor of the people, and in that light, razing the Domus Aurea seemed like a good idea. What they then did with the vacant land it created was a prime example of symbolic politics, for which the entire world is still grateful, judging by the daily, modern-day long lines: they built the largest amphitheater the world had ever seen, for the people of Rome—after all, all the people wanted were circuses (and bread). Rome's new arena was officially called the Amphitheatrum Flavium, after the family of the builders. Its now much more famous nickname, the Colosseum, did not pass from the statue (the *colossus*) onto the amphitheater until after the year 1000. Vespasian, the first of the Flavian emperors, thought that Nero's colossal statue could remain, in a modified form. When Beda the monk wrote the famous words, "*Quamdiu stabit coliseus, stabit et Roma; quando cadet coliseus, cadet et Roma; quando cadet Roma, cadet et mundus*," in the seventh century, he was not talking about the amphitheater, which much later came to symbolize Rome: "As long as the colossus stands, Rome will stand; should the colossus fall, so will Rome; if Rome falls, so will the world."

Strangely enough, the most enormous and striking reminder of Nero and his administration escaped, in a roundabout way, the *damnatio memoriae*, and his name will live on forever in one of the most visited places in Rome today. What remained of the Domus Aurea after its destruction lies beneath the surface, but it was also built over by a thermae complex of yet a later emperor, Trajan. The remnants of the latter building can be found above ground, in the Parco del Colle Oppio, on the Viale della Domus Aurea. Standing on top of what remains of the Domus Aurea, between Trajan's thermae and the Flavian amphitheater, the first century of the empire comes closer, both visibly and invisibly. Given this backdrop, the notion that Augustus alone dramatically changed the appearance of Rome recedes quickly.

XVII

PIAZZA DEI PROTOMARTIRI

NERO'S CIRCUS AND THE BIRTH OF SAINT PETER'S

In ancient Rome, whoever left the city in a northwestern direction walked along the old Via Cornelia (no longer there) toward the so-called Ager Vaticanus, a piece of land named after the Vatican Hill. It lay just outside the urban area, and during the early Imperial Period, at the time of the Julio-Claudians, there were graves and little else, at first. Much later, Emperor Hadrian had his mausoleum built along this route. The site has been well preserved and is now known as the Castel Sant'Angelo. It was Caligula, successor of Tiberius and emperor of Rome between 37 and 41, who built a stadium along the Via Cornelia, in the style of the Circus Maximus, intended for chariot racing and other spectacles. After the Great Fire of 64, when Nero needed a large number of scapegoats and blamed the Christians, he used the Circus of Caligula primarily to have them tortured to death during public persecutions. The street sign that recalls these early ("proto-") Christian martyrs is found within the walls of current Vatican City: Piazza dei Protomartiri. The square is located—not coincidentally—near the entrance of the Ufficio Scavi, the headquarters of the archaeology department that is in charge of what lies buried beneath St. Peter's Basilica.

By far the most well-known Christian who was tortured and executed in the Circus of Nero, during the paranoia of 64, was Simon Peter, one of the twelve disciples of Jesus, considered by Catholics the first Pope of Rome. Reportedly at his own request, Peter was nailed to the cross upside down by the Roman executioners. The reason for his unusual request is unclear: he either considered himself not worthy of dying the same way Jesus had, or he wanted to make a symbolic gesture. As Jesus' first apostle, Peter had quite a few followers, who reportedly witnessed his public execution in the stadium. Following the execution of their leader, Peter's followers erected a simple tomb for him, in accordance with Christian customs, along the Via Cornelia on the Vatican Hill. Initially, it was probably not much more than a hole in the ground. Peter's fame spread among the followers of Jesus Christ, resulting in a modest monument about one hundred years after his death, to better mark the location of the grave and perhaps to prevent it from being covered by new tombs.

Constantine the Great was the first Roman emperor to allow the ever-growing Christian community to stay. In the fourth century, he came up with a plan to replace St. Peter's modest commemorative monument with a larger church. He had the ground of the cemetery prepared, which included incorporating the existing tombs of both heathen Romans and early Christians into the foundations of the new commemorative monument. The church Constantine built would function for more than eleven centuries, but after deterioration and subsequent frantic restoration attempts, it had to be demolished in 1506. The sixteenth century had barely begun, the Italian Renaissance was in full swing, and the Catholic Church was more powerful than ever. Of course a new church had to be built, but the basilica's size and appearance were still topics for discussion. Then came several decades of making blueprints and revisions, of building and subsequent demolitions—a process involving, in order of appearance, Bramante, Raphael, Michelangelo, and Bernini. The result was astounding: exactly on the spot where the apostle Peter was reportedly given a simple burial place in 64 CE, a grandiose, impressive basilica had arisen, with dimensions that exceeded everyone's imagination: Saint Peter's was (re)born.

The special and at times bizarre history of the location that is marked by the largest Catholic church in the world represents for many archaeologists and aficionados the greatest attraction of the Vatican today. This is undoubtedly because it became possible to descend personally (led by a guide of the Ufficio Scavi) to the city of the dead that lies hidden deep below the immense basilica. The significance of the place for the Roman Catholic Church, and hence for a substantial part of the world population, is mostly felt above ground, through the steady flow of pilgrims. But it is in the deepest catacombs of St. Peter's Basilica, tens of feet below Michelangelo's dome and Bernini's canopy, that the soul of this place comes to life. The countless urns in alcoves, the burial chambers, and the archaeological stratigraphy laid bare for the naked eye to see present you that history, layer by layer. It is a history that started, very simply, in an everyday place: a Roman cemetery. The dead, buried in staid pits, coffins, and alcoves, address the visitors directly in areas where they left an inscription behind. But they are completely unaware of the global interest their eternal resting place has enjoyed, and of the (art-) historical riches that would come to rest on their shoulders centuries later.

XVIII

VIA SACRA

FORUM ROMANUM: FROM TITUS TO SEPTIMIUS SEVERUS

Nero brought down his own dynasty, not actively but simply by not appointing a successor. After a tumultuous but brief period of successive claims to the throne (the so-called Year of the Four Emperors), the Flavians successfully kept the emperor's crown for several generations. The three emperors—Vespasian and his sons, Titus and Domitian—ruled between 69 and 96 CE. In the seventies, Vespasian ordered the construction of the Colosseum; his sons finished the job. The Amphitheatrum Flavium was intended mostly for popular entertainment—spectacles such as gladiator fights, reenactments of sea battles, and public executions. It was the first permanent stone arena in Rome—before, temporary wooden stadiums were used. And, of course, it was the largest in the entire empire. In addition to being the period of Colosseum construction, the Flavian quarter-century was also an era of events with far-reaching consequences, such as the Revolt of the Batavi, the eruption of Vesuvius, and the First Jewish-Roman War. Titus' triumphal arch commemorates this war. It marks the transition between today's Piazza del Colosseo and the lower part of the Forum Romanum.

Does the (modern) sign VIA SACRA, on the southwest side of the Colosseum, toward Titus' arch, really mark the place of the immemorial Sacred Road along which the triumphal marches led to the Capitoline? If there is one place in Rome where the archaeological stratigraphy is a hodgepodge of reconstructions, layer upon layer, it would be on and around the Forum Romanum. If a layperson wants to get a good feel for ancient Rome during one specific period—the early or later Imperial Period, the Republic—the forum may be the least suitable place to pay an (unprepared) visit, or in any case the most confusing. The Via Sacra, or, as sources refer to it most often, the Sacra Via, is the oldest and most famous street in Rome and runs through the Forum Romanum. It started at the highest point of the Velia, a hill that the Romans had already partially leveled and that Mussolini stripped further. The Velian Hill basically covered the space between the Palatine and the Colle Oppio; you can still get a partial view of the differences in height when you are standing to the west of the Colosseum, at Titus' arch and the temple of Venus and Roma. Before Nero built his Domus Aurea, the hill must have been a little taller than what you see there.

From the foot of Titus' arch, you can look down on the entire Forum Romanum. If you look behind you, in the direction of the Colosseum, you will see hints of height differences in "street levels" in the forum. They are the result of excavations and many demolition and building projects: on one side you see the street level as it was at the time of Augustus (who renovated many buildings on the forum), and on the other you see the street level as it was in Nero's days (logically, the latter is higher). During Nero's reign, in 66, the Jews in Judea revolted, resulting in the First Jewish-Roman War. Nero sent his best general, Vespasian, to Judea, and he managed to quell the insurrection. It was not until years later (Nero was dead and Vespasian was emperor) that Titus took Jerusalem, the capital, by brute force. The city and the temple of the Jews were ransacked. Titus returned to Rome with loads of booty and, reportedly, at least ten thousand prisoners of war. Most Jewish slaves were put to work: after all, a huge amphitheater was being built in Rome. The remainder of what Titus had brought home (temple treasures, such as a menorah) is displayed on the famous reliefs on Titus' arch. The emperor himself is on it, too, being led through Rome in his chariot. This triumphal parade took place in 71, along the Via Sacra, as was customary. The arch of Titus is adorned with reliefs about this triumph, but it is not the real *triumphal* arch, built to commemorate the victory, contrary to what most people assume. That arch did exist, but it was elsewhere, near the eastern bend of the Circus Maximus. How do historians know this? The arch on the Forum Romanum shows the apotheosis, Titus' ascent into heaven, and the inscription reads that the *deified* Titus and Vespasian are being honored. That could not have been written until after the death of the emperor. It follows that this arch was erected to honor Titus (it was indeed commissioned by his brother, and successor, Domitian). The actual triumphal arch of Titus, the one from the Circus Maximus, is even depicted in small on the relief.

Both Vespasian and Domitian remodeled this section of the Velia, where Nero had built his Domus Aurea (as "Vespasian's Forum"). The colossus from the former entrance hall of Nero's palace was allowed to stay, but it was given a facelift and the attributes of Helios or Sol; from now on it would depict Titus as the sun god. The ancient sources do not reveal exactly how that happened. Was it literally a facelift, chopping off Nero's head and replacing it with a new one (as Emperor Commodus would do later)? It is more likely that the statue had just not been finished yet and that it was relatively easy to give it Titus' traits. Lastly, that head was given a halo, and perhaps immediately also a whip—a reference to Sol as driver of the sun chariot.

Nero had redirected the course of the Via Sacra to the square with his colossus, the current place of the Santa Francesca Romana (where parts of the base of the statue were found). However, during nineteenth-century excavations Nero's pavement was removed. Only in the nineteenth century did they start excavating and mapping the ruins on the Forum Romanum. In the course of the centuries, the monuments had become overgrown; during the Middle Ages, the forum was even given the nickname Campo Vaccino, "cattle field," for the deserted grazing field it had become. Nineteenth-century archaeologist Giacomo Boni fought hard to get the Forum Romanum awarded the protected status of an archaeological park.

Domitian died a dramatic death: he was murdered in his own palace in a conspiracy that probably included his wife. The Senate then appointed his successor, the sexagenarian Nerva, who had always been loyal to the Flavians. Nerva would turn out to be an interim emperor. He adopted the successful commander Trajan, thus making him crown prince. Thus began a period often heralded as that of the "adoption emperors" or the "good emperors." Trajan, for example, came to be considered a "model emperor" after his death. His military successes are celebrated on a column covered in reliefs (also his burial chamber) on the forum down the road, on the Via dei Fori Imperiali.

Hadrian, who succeeded him as emperor, focused more on consolidation than on expansion of Roman power. There are three spots in Rome where Hadrian's legacy is still visible: at the Pantheon, which he rebuilt into its current shape; at the Castel Sant'Angelo, which he built as his mausoleum; and in the east corner of the Forum Romanum, on the Velia. The remnants of the temple of Venus and Roma that Hadrian built there still hint at how impressive the building must have been (the current columns belong to the porticus that was erected around the temple). He moved the colossus for it (reportedly using twenty-four elephants)—to a lower spot closer to the Colosseum. The temple was larger than the remaining columns suggest: the Santa Francesca Romana was built in one part of it. In contrast to most temples on the Forum Romanum, which only featured steps and an entrance in the front, Hadrian built the temple of Venus and Roma entirely in Greek style—accessible from all sides. He was known to be a great admirer of Greek art and culture. Hadrian's successor, Antoninus Pius, would also be remembered as one of the "good emperors." He, too, built a temple on the Via Sacra—there is a reason they called it "sacred." He did so after the death of his wife Faustina (in 141), and he dedicated the building to her. Any visitor can attest to the fact that relatively little is preserved of the so-called temple of Antoninus Pius and Faustina, because it was later turned into a church. On the forum, no trace of the administration of emperor-philosopher Marcus Aurelius, who succeeded Antoninus Pius, can be found today. His son and successor Commodus, who, contrary to his father, was mainly known for his cruelty and was no longer seen as one of the "good emperors," erected a pillar for Marcus Aurelius, which is still in its original place on the Field of Mars, along the current Via del Corso. The triumphal arch on the side of the Capitoline of the Forum Romanum shows how Septimius Severus restored order to an empire that had been divided following the death of Commodus. This impressive triumphal arch was a gift from the Senate to Septimius Severus, in honor of his victories in the ancient Near East toward the end of the second century. Originally the emperor was on top, in a triumphal chariot. Julia Domna, Septimius Severus' wife, ordered the renovation of the complex of Vestal Virgins on the Forum Romanum, and today we can still admire what she left behind.

The remnants of the temple of Vesta, the goddess served by the Vestal priestesses, still show that it was a round sanctuary. It was located on the Via Sacra, together with the House of the Vestal Virgins, which held work and living spaces. This originally consisted of both a section for the Vestal Virgins and a room for the highest ranking (male) priest, the Domus Publica. Following the end of the Republic, the emperor himself fulfilled the role of *pontifex maximus* ("highest priest"); for reasons of convenience, Augustus moved the seat to the Palatine. The Vestal Virgins stayed, however, and served the goddess Vesta, usually for thirty years. They dedicated themselves to keeping her fire eternally burning and safeguarding the important state acts (in the

Regia, long ago the official dwelling of the king of Rome) and cult objects. They had to swear a strict vow of chastity, but they lived otherwise comfortable lives and enjoyed all sorts of privileges normally not accorded to women. After thirty years they were allowed to leave the convent and marry if they so desired, but some voluntarily stayed and served Vesta for life. To be considered for the Vestal priesthood, women needed not only to have an impressive ancestry but also to be fairly bright. The responsibility bestowed on them was too important to leave to less-intelligent daughters of the wealthy. On the other hand, the punishments were horrific. The most notorious (in antiquity and now) was the punishment for breaking the chastity vow. In accordance with the law, the Vestal Virgin who broke her vow was buried alive in a specially arranged underground space on the outskirts of the city. This was the sad fate of Cornelia, for example, a priestess of Vesta under Domitian. It is said that she audibly maintained she was innocent until her death.

At some point, the Via Sacra also had numerous other buildings. You can witness the remnants today while walking over the centuries-old cobblestones. There are examples of very old places of worship, which the Romans had revered since the Regal Period, although they did not know exactly why, such as the Black Stone (*Lapis Niger*). Among the oldest temples on the forum were those of Saturn and of Castor and Pollux, as well as the temple dedicated to Concordia. The halls for the Senate and people's meetings, the *curia* and the *comitium*, respectively, are also part of the oldest remnants on the forum. The two basilicas, Julia and Aemilia, on the sides of the forum, evoke memories of Rome in the Republican Period, during which ambitious members of prominent families acted as architects (although emperor Augustus had a hand in both buildings, too). Basilicas were very popular in the Republic: they enabled all sorts of daily activities—from shopping to civil court cases—in any kind of weather.

Septimius Severus' arch marks the end of our walk across the Augustinian pavement of the Via Sacra. If you look up at the arch, you may try to make out the long inscription it features. It says that it was erected for Septimius Severus and his son Caracalla. Originally it held another name, that is, before Caracalla falsified history by deleting it: Geta. After his last victory, Septimius Severus made his eldest son, Caracalla, co-emperor, and Geta, his youngest, was appointed successor to the throne. After Septimius' death, a dramatic family history unfolded: Caracalla had his little brother removed. By now, history had taught the Romans what would happen next; they started to prepare for a new era of tyranny.

XIX

VIALE DELLE TERME DI CARACALLA

BATHING AND WELLNESS IN A FILTHY CITY

In ancient Rome, there was a bathhouse on just about every street corner. A visit to the bathhouse was a necessity—two thousand years ago, life in a busy metropolis could make you quite dirty. Some wealthy Romans could afford the luxury of a private bathhouse, but most people had to resort to public baths. Even well-to-do Romans liked going to the public bathhouses: it was a social activity that most people enjoyed very much. The really enormous public bathhouses, the *thermae*, were built during the Imperial Period (commissioned by the emperors themselves), such as those of Trajan (on top of the foundations of Nero's Domus Aurea) and of the later emperor Diocletian (near the Stazione Termini). We walk away from the old center for a bit, in order to get an impression of the original dimensions of a Roman *thermae* complex, toward the Viale delle Terme di Caracalla.

The ruins of the *thermae* of Caracalla, which can be found along this street, are an impressive spectacle. The gigantic bathhouse was built parallel to the Via Appia. It was commissioned by Caracalla and his father, Septimius Severus. An inscription from Late Antiquity calls it the Thermae Antoninianae (Caracallae)—after the Antoninian family that had adopted Septimius Severus. The family's intentions were not to create some sort of exorbitantly chic bathroom for themselves; Roman bathhouses were public buildings, and access was both a public and a societal good. Like in other Roman bathhouses, the three main bathhouse spaces in the *thermae* of Caracalla were the *frigidarium* (featuring a cold bath), the *tepidarium* (with heated walls and floor), and the *caldarium* (containing hot-water baths). But there was also an open-air pool (*natatio*) and some splash pools scattered around the complex.

It was a relatively new design, typical for the later Imperial Period, in which all the baths had some sort of "gymnasiums" (*palaestra*) on the sides, places for sports, gymnastics, and weight training. And there was more: the gigantic complex also housed libraries, a theater, and vast green gardens. If you close your eyes, you may be able to imagine, between the ruins, the marble decorations on the walls, the brightly colored murals surrounding you, the immense mosaics on the floor under your feet, and the enormous sculptures you would encounter in the hallways. All this is gone today. What remains of the interior is in museums, on squares, and in parks inside and outside Rome.

Yet the ruins of Caracalla's *thermae* have been incredibly well preserved. They withstood the 847 earthquake and the ravages of the Middle Ages relatively well. After that, they sunk into oblivion, and the remnants disappeared under plant growth and construction. Not until Farnese Pope Paul III did the remnants resurface, but this was rather unfortunate, actually: excavations in 1546 partially destroyed the *thermae*. The Pope was mainly looking for antique pieces of art to embellish his Palazzo Farnese. He did find those: beautiful and famous sculptures such as *The Farnese Bull* and the *Farnese Hercules* became valuable additions to his art collection. These and other sculptures are now in the archaeological museum in Naples. Large granite containers, of Egyptian origin, which were used as bathtubs in Caracalla's *thermae* complex, today adorn the Piazza Farnese, just southwest of the Piazza Navona. At least until the mid-sixteenth century, the square only had one of the two bathtubs. Because of its resemblance, another tub, originally on the Piazza San Marco, was moved to the Piazza Farnese in the second half of the sixteenth century—as decoration for the square. In 1626, Giacomo Rainaldi first filled the tubs with water again by hooking them up to the Acqua Paola; he turned them into fountains that are still there today.

XX

VIALE CASTRENSE

A SECOND COLOSSEUM IN ROME

A stroll along the remnants of the Aurelian Wall can take a full day. It will be a hot journey, certainly in the summer, under a mercilessly cloudless sky. But it will be more than worth the effort; there are few Roman undertakings that will aid you more in clarifying the image of the dimensions of the old city. Built by Emperor Aurelian, this city wall is still standing (although not in its original form everywhere) for the most part today, and it can still be followed fairly accurately. If you are ever crazy enough to undertake that journey, as I did, then you will be walking around the Rome of later antiquity. It is odd how the most unexpected and simplest undertakings can sharpen your idea of a historic place or event more than hours of study could. You can experience for yourself that, toward the end of the third century, one could walk all the way around the city of Rome in a single day. From the Viale delle Terme di Caracalla we will now follow the Aurelian Wall and its history, in a northeastern direction, toward "Rome's second Colosseum."

The impetus for the construction of the new defense walls around 275 was the difficult period the city and the empire endured. After Caracalla (who died a violent death in 217), the Severian dynasty remained in power for a few more decades, but history would know the third century mainly as a century of crisis, with an impressively long list of "soldier emperors" who followed one another in rapid succession. At the same time, quite a few self-proclaimed counter-emperors came up. At times, nobody could tell who the usurper was. They would be in power for such a short period of time, and their base would be so fragile that they would often only commission a few construction activities in their name. To a certain extent they left the capital of the empire untouched. One of the few leading figures in this century who did have an impact was Aurelian, proclaimed emperor by his soldiers on the battlefield but subsequently also recognized as such by the Senate in Rome. The most noticeable legacy of his principate, which lasted a mere five years, was the construction of a new wall around the city. The unrelenting internal strife for the throne had weakened the empire, leaving it vulnerable to attacks by northern tribes—the new walls weren't seen as a project of prestige but rather of unavoidable necessity.

The new city wall would be about twelve miles long. The construction had to start without delay, and so wherever possible buildings were integrated into the wall. That was cheap and easy: why would you first demolish a robust structure only to rebuild it? Integration into the Aurelian Wall, which is what happened with the Pyramid of Cestius, came with a pleasant side effect for historians: the buildings chosen for this purpose were spared demolition and oblivion. When Emperor Aurelian built his wall around Rome, he also came upon the Amphitheatrum Castrense—a kind of mini Colosseum, virtually unknown to the public at large today. The Aurelian Wall has remained reasonably unscathed here, at the intersection of the Via Nola and the Viale Castrense (not even that far from the "real" Colosseum). The Amphitheatrum Castrense, which lent the street its name, is far from unscathed but still very visible.

The Amphitheatrum Castrense was probably built in the third century, during the reign of Emperor Septimius Severus or of a later descendant in the Severian dynasty, Elagabalus. The exterior wall originally featured three floors with open arches, but the arena could seat far fewer spectators than the Colosseum down the road; it must have been one of the imperial residences and therefore mainly used for private shows for the imperial family and its court, not for the people of Rome. The theater's nickname, "Castrense," is derived from the Latin word *castrum*, originally meaning "(army) camp" and suggestive of a (partial) military role. In fact, it is not entirely certain (but whatever is, in archaeology?) that the round building on the Via Castrense is the Amphitheatrum Castrense. This identification has been generally accepted, but it is based on two notions: the current structure is located on the exact same spot as an amphitheater marked on an old map of Rome, and the assumption that the word *castrum* also meant something like "imperial dwelling" or "court." This would naturally imply such a dwelling was part of the Amphitheatrum Castrense.

Excavations have brought to light that the Santa Croce in Gerusalemme—the church behind the Amphitheatrum Castrense, seen from the Via Nola––was built on top of a large complex of imperial areas. As mentioned, those areas date back to the time of Septimius Severus, but its most famous inhabitant did not move in until the early fourth century; that was Helena, the mother of Emperor Constantine the Great. Both mother and son converted to Christianity. The story goes that, on a trip around the eastern part of the Roman Empire, Helena found, among many relics, a wooden cross that turned out to be the "True Cross" on which Jesus had died. She actually found three True Crosses, but nothing happened when a dying woman tested the first two crosses for Helena by lying down on them. Only when she touched the third cross did she immediately recover from her illness. Hence the name the "True Cross," which is at least an indication that a considerable "trade" in Christian relics had begun as early as the fourth century. Helena brought the True Cross home to Rome, where it has remained until today. By the way, there were quite a few more versions of that "True Cross" around. In the Middle Ages the number had reportedly gone up so high that in the sixteenth century

John Calvin remarked bitterly that the wood from all those cross relics together would be enough to build an entire ship.

Helena kept Jesus' cross in her own palace for safekeeping. Of course she thought it actually deserved a more solid and fitting home. So she turned the modest chapel in her home into a church, which later became a pilgrimage site for Christians the world over thanks to the importance of this relic. The sacred repository of the True Cross was given the name Santa Croce in Gerusalemme (the Holy Cross in Jerusalem) and became one of the seven pilgrimage churches of Rome. That church still attracts a few visitors and pilgrims, but its appearance has changed in the course of centuries. In the thirteenth century, the Santa Croce in Gerusalemme underwent a few renovations, and the more Baroque style of the facade you can still see today dates back to the eighteenth century.

Walking past the Amphitheatrum Castrense toward the Santa Croce in Gerusalemme, if we go inside for a moment, we see that the story of Helena finding the True Cross in Jerusalem is depicted once more behind the altar. Unfortunately, the section of the gardens with the archaeological remains of the Amphitheatrum Castrense is hardly ever open to the public—and when it is, you must be accompanied by a guide from the church. However, from the outside you can very clearly see how the structure was incorporated into the Aurelian Wall: all the access archways to the arena were sealed shut. The gigantic, twelve-mile-long fencing-in of Rome was a desperate attempt by Emperor Aurelian to keep numerous "barbarian" tribes out, but its construction also represented the writing on the wall for Rome: it would not be long until the Aurelian Wall no longer offered any resistance either.

XXI

PONTE MILVIO

IN THE NAME OF THE CROSS

On October 28, 312, a momentous confrontation took place. Emperor Maxentius, whom many called "the usurper," and his troops were facing Constantine and his army. Both camps had met on the battlefield several times, but the most important battle was still to come and would take place in Rome. Maxentius gathered his men on the north side of the Via Flaminia, just outside the Aurelian Wall. The promising and ambitious general Constantine was keenly aware that control over the Western Roman Empire would be his in case of a victory. That division of the empire into East and West would become more pronounced from this moment on. During the reign of Constantine, he saw to it that Byzantium would replace Rome as the heart and capital of the empire. The "new Rome" was even named after him: Constantinople.

Yet many traces left by Constantine can be found not only in Istanbul but also in Rome. Most well known is the Arch of Constantine, simply because it is right next to the Colosseum. That triumphal arch features quite a few *spolia*—decorative structures stripped from other, older monuments and "reused." On Constantine's arch we find *spolia* from the days of Trajan, Hadrian, and Marcus Aurelius. It seems that this is how Constantine sought to position himself within the tradition of those "good emperors." The integrity of those old Roman emperors, whose reputations had been established and were positive in Constantine's time, was thus given new meaning, and on his triumphal arch, Constantine is equated with that virtue. Whether he himself was responsible for that is not entirely clear. After all, the triumphal arch was a tribute to Constantine, offered to him by the Senate. The triumph to which the arch was dedicated took place on that very October 28, 312, on a bridge four miles north: the Ponte Milvio.

The bridge had just been replaced—at the request of Maxentius no less—by a temporary ship's bridge, and it wasn't very stable. Constantine had considerably fewer troops and seemed to have little chance. His later biographer, Eusebius, writes that Constantine felt invigorated when he had a vision on October 27. Up in the clear sky, a cross appeared with the words "*in hoc signo vinces*," or, "by this sign you will conquer." The following day, he did indeed win: Maxentius' army stormed the bridge, which collapsed. The men drowned en masse in the Tiber, including their leader. Maxentius' body was recovered from the river the day after the Battle of the Ponte Milvio, to be decapitated as yet. Thus began a narrative that would be told for a long time to come: for the first time in the history of mankind, a military battle was won in the name of the Christian cross. Constantine became emperor and would later become known as "the Great."

Although Constantine did indeed convert to the Christian faith and pursue a pro-Christian policy (following a period of systematic Christian persecution), Christianity did not become the state religion until later (under Theodosius). The Constantine era is often viewed as a kind of transition period: Constantine is often (or readily) considered good, but for the most part, Rome itself actually fared poorly starting in the fourth century. These are value judgments with lots of ifs and buts, and maybe we don't even need them to provide a clear picture of the slow but steady decline that led to the inevitable fall of the Western Roman Empire. In the past, Constantine's impact on the history of Rome (and Europe) was often a bit exaggerated. Of course this is linked to how history, and then especially that of Christianity, unfolded. One cannot clearly interpret history based on today's insight, no matter how difficult it is to disregard that insight. Although the impact and the innovative character of the reign of Constantine were often a bit overestimated, in hindsight his choice of Christianity, a monotheistic religion, was a very important one: after him, all emperors were Christians, except for Julian (the Apostate).

In form and appearance, the city of Rome actually remained fairly "heathen" under Constantine. The many temples in the center stayed intact and would only be definitively abandoned much later. The same goes for the philosophical schools. Constantine's own building plans were concentrated mainly in the periphery of Rome. He erected monuments on the graves of both Peter (now Saint Peter's) and Paul (now San Paolo fuori le Mura), the founders of the Church. On the other side of the city, the Santa Croce in Gerusalemme rose up thanks to the empress mother, and right next to it, in the Lateran Palace, which was the private property of Constantine, Jesus was worshiped as *salvatore* (savior). Constantine was the first emperor to leave the Palatine behind and move with his court to the Palazzo Lateranense. The entire complex was later donated to the Church, which transformed the palazzo into a religious patriarchate. Constantine built a church there, too, later known as San Giovanni in Laterano, originally (and actually still officially) called Santissimo Salvatore, even though nothing remains of the original building. From that moment on, the church and the palazzo on the current Piazza di San Giovanni in Laterano were the places where the popes of Rome resided. It would stay that way until the popes were expelled from Rome in the fourteenth century.

In the Constantine era, Christian services no longer needed to take place in hidden "house churches." This resulted in a new trend within architecture, consisting of the construction of churches and monuments for martyrs. Another architectural trend from the age of Constantine would leave an even greater mark on the building history of Rome: *spolia* became an almost certain and inevitable part of new construction projects. Decorative elements and expensive materials from old, pagan monuments would be used in the construction of churches from now on, a practice that reappears in almost all old churches of Rome. So, construction in the Eternal City did not stop. Despite the foundation of the "new Rome" on the Bosporus, for now, Rome on the Tiber kept its name and fame. Its position as political center of the world had run its course, however.

XXII

PASSETTO DI BORGO

THE HIDDEN STREET OF THE POPES

Pilgrim and nonbeliever alike will be moved the first time they stand at the beginning of the Via della Conciliazione, ready to walk the last few steps toward the immeasurable St. Peter's Basilica and the welcoming embrace of the monumental square. That direct, panoramic route hits home (exactly the way Mussolini intended). However, visitors enter from the other side almost as often, arriving at the square from the Ottaviano metro stop, through the side wings of the theatrical square, and passing under Bernini's baldachin. These pillars mark the boundary between Vatican City and Italy, but this is also the spot where an old, seemingly medieval, and relatively high wall runs parallel to Bernini's baldachin and then follows the path of the Via della Conciliazione. From the outside it looks like some sort of defense structure. Nothing suggests that we are looking at a hidden, covered walkway. Rome's most well-hidden street is known as the *passetto*, the "small passageway." The secret corridor takes you from Saint Peter's to the Castel Sant'Angelo, half a mile away. For whom was this strange, secret passage built?

The eastern part of the Roman Empire, with Constantinople as its capital, strengthened its position after Constantine's rule, and it would exert its power for centuries. In Rome, however, several attacks by so-called barbaric tribes permanently subverted power in the course of the fifth century. Chaos and a series of sieges followed; the situation became untenable. In 476, Odoaker, leader of the Germanic tribes, removed the last emperor, Romulus Augustus. Rome fell, and so did the Western Roman Empire, exhausted and having been subjected to a long series of attacks and lootings. In the sixth century, the city fell into the hands of the Goths until *their* empire fell, too. When the Lombards settled in Italy, they adopted practically nothing of Roman culture. Rome was in ruins, and there was no emperor or senate to restore the public order. For more than a millennium, the city had thrived, during a large part of which it was the beating heart of a global empire. How the empire could succumb, slowly but permanently, has been a topic of debate for as long as we can remember. What is certain, however, is that no single factor was the decisive one. As is almost always the case in history, there was a complex combination of causes and circumstances. It is also certain that the chaos in Rome remained for a long time. At that time, discord reigned in Europe.

The city plan of Rome was not left untouched during this period. In 546, when the Goths recaptured Rome from the Byzantines, their destructive leader Totila fortunately did not keep his promise of turning Rome into one large pasture for grazing. He did destroy a large section of the city walls, including the Mausoleum of Hadrian (the monument we now know as the Castel Sant'Angelo, the Castle of the Holy Angel). Emperor Aurelian had incorporated part of that mausoleum into his Aurelian Wall, and from that moment on, Hadrian's eternal peace was forever disturbed: the vault would serve as a castle, and in turbulent times it was mainly used in the defense of Rome. That is, until a miracle happened toward the end of the sixth century.

Rome was suffering from a terrible plague of epidemic proportions, to which even the Pope (Pelagius II) fell victim, in 590. His successor, Gregory I, nicknamed "the Great," organized a special procession, a supplication to God, to drive the plague out of the city. When the parade of devoted, pleading believers had almost reached Saint Peter's, Gregory saw the archangel Michael appear in the sky, directly over the Mausoleum of Hadrian, with a sword in his hand. Baffled, Gregory kept staring up at the sky, and the next moment

Michael put the sword in the scabbard. Gregory interpreted this as a sign that the prayers had been answered, and indeed, the plague left Rome. The story of this divine miracle was told for centuries, and a statue of Michael with his sword was placed on top of the mausoleum in 1536. The statue is still there in the Castel Sant'Angelo, although the angel on the roof now is an eighteenth-century version.

Not until around 800 was the need felt to rebuild the walls destroyed by Totila. The period in between, roughly from the seventh until the ninth century, is one of which a tourist in Rome will see very little, and hear even less. For city historians, these centuries mark a time on which—perhaps due to a lack of clear leaders with grand building plans—it is hard to get a grip. For this period, we do have a few exceptional sources: the so-called pilgrimage guides that started to emerge in the seventh century. They convey a history, not of emperors or popes, but of humble, traveling believers in search of salvation or healing. The impact on the city's history by this growing number of travelers to Rome might have been larger than that of the early popes, or even than that of any single emperor who converted to Christianity. Although the trip must have been dangerous and expensive, these travelers came to Rome of their own accord. The rising flow of pilgrims was born from the fervent wish to be near the graves and remains of saints and martyrs who had gained fame all over Europe. The construction inspired by this interest gave Rome a new boost.

We cannot simply call these pilgrims the first "tourists" in Rome, since in just about every aspect they were different from today's tourists. The pilgrimage often did not even lead them to the center of Rome, but mainly to the tombs of saints on the outskirts of the city, outside the walls. Saint Peter's tomb was often the ending or starting point, and Paul's tomb was also always on the list. But in other places around Rome there were more tombs of saints to be found, often in miles-long subterranean hallways, the so-called catacombs. The fact that they were underground was more or less a necessity:

due to the growing number of Christians, interment began to replace cremation, and land available for graves became scarcer—and so Christians opted for underground burials. But in the sixth and seventh centuries, those subterranean hallways were neither wide enough nor safe enough to accommodate the growing number of visiting pilgrims. Therefore, graves were removed around the most important martyrs' graves; the grounds were evened, and churches were built. Examples are the San Lorenzo fuori le Mura and Sant'Agnese, east of the wall, the Santi Nereo e Achilleo in the south, the San Pancrazio on the Janiculum in the west, and the San Valentino on the Via Flaminia, north of the wall.

Since the time of Charlemagne, the Pope in Rome had become more than the shepherd-in-chief of his flock of believers in the city. Charlemagne's father, Pepin the Short, had come to Rome's aid, in exchange for the papal blessing, when he was king of the Franks. Pepin the Short expelled the Lombards from Italy. He gave the Pope control over a number of cities in central Italy, which was, in fact, the birth of the Papal State. Charlemagne had Leo III crown him emperor in Saint Peter's Church in Rome, in December of the year 800. He was declared *imperator* and *augustus* of a new political alliance that had developed in Western Europe following the fall of Rome, the Sacro Romano Impero—the Holy Roman Empire (although Byzantine emperors stayed in power, too). Charlemagne hated the coronation ritual, originating from his father's wish to receive the papal blessing, since the one being crowned is by definition lower in rank than the one crowning him. The "gift" of the emperor's title remained a symbol of the dependency on the Pope in the following centuries.

In any case, Rome became the religious center of the new Roman Empire, and Saint Peter's (where the popes themselves and their administrations still resided) turned into a pilgrimage site, which had to be adequately protected. Defensewise, a few things needed to be done, especially following the death of Charlemagne and the fragmentation of his empire. The Saracens from the Middle East had made a name for themselves in Europe as notorious pirates and looters. This was one of the reasons that, under Pope Leo IV's leadership in the ninth century, for the first time a defense structure that enclosed the entire Vatican was built around Saint Peter's: the *civitas leonina*.

In the meantime, the pilgrims kept coming, including in the ninth, tenth, and following centuries. Beginning in the eighth and ninth centuries, the churches within the city walls became more and more regular parts of the Roman pilgrimage. One of the reasons for this was the Church's easing of its "bones policy"; whereas initially "disturbing" the remains of saints was strictly forbidden, moving them was now tolerated. In the course of the centuries it became clear that the contents of many graves outside the walls would be safer within the walls. There, they could at least be protected against looting. During this time, many relics ended up in the newly built crypts of the churches of Rome. Perhaps all that dragging of sacred bones contributed to the growing mistrust expressed by pilgrims in the twelfth century; they increasingly wondered whether all those remains were really located in the relic shrines in front of which they were kneeling so devotedly. This skepticism was also one of the causes behind a kind of relics competition that started between churches—mainly between the Lateran and the Vatican.

Meanwhile in Europe, the times were still turbulent. From the eleventh century on, popes were elected by cardinals: religious leaders, not political leaders, assigned religious offices. This eventually led to the Investiture Controversy, which occurred around the same time city-states in northern Italy gained their independence. But the authority of the Pope and of the Catholic Church was far from being universally accepted, and the conflict came to a head when Pope Gregory VII and Emperor Henry IV were involved in a dispute. Some time later, in the thirteenth century, Pope

Nicholas III (1277–1280) feared for his life so gravely that he moved from the Lateran palace to the Vatican *palazzi* and decided to create an emergency escape route. On top of the wall of the *civitas leonina*, which ran to the easily defensible Castel Sant'Angelo, he built a walkway. This was the origin of the viaduct nicknamed Passetto di Borgo. Centuries later, in 1492, Borgia Pope Alexander VI did his part by adding a new layer that transformed the Passetto into the covered gallery you can still recognize today.

Nicholas III had good foresight. In 1527, his escape route saved a pope's life when, on May 6, the infamous Sacco di Roma ("Sack of Rome") took place—the looting of the city by an army of German and Spanish mercenaries led by Charles V. The city was shaken, and Pope Clement VII had to run to save his life. It is said that a loyal Swiss Guard accompanied him through the *passetto*, with only a torch in his hand to light the narrow passage. The escape route led via stairs to underground bunkers near the Castel Sant'Angelo, where he spent many fearful hours. To make the remainder of a possible stay more pleasant, early-sixteenth-century popes added loggias, reception halls, counsel rooms, papal apartments, and even a chapel to the Castel Sant'Angelo.

In the sixteenth century, the wall of the *passetto* cut the Borgo neighborhood in two when a new wall parallel to the old one was built: the Borgo Vecchio on one side and the Borgo Nuovo on the other. Several new gates and passageways were added on that occasion. During this time of relative calm and prosperity, the Castel Sant'Angelo was transformed from a papal shelter into a prison. Its most recent modification came from Pope Urban VIII, who had the upper gallery of Alexander VI covered as well. Today, the *passetto* is closed; only on rare occasions, and by appointment, is a tourist allowed in. Fortunately, you can get a very good view of the popes' hidden passageway from the roof of the Castel Sant'Angelo and the dome of Saint Peter's.

XXIII

PIAZZA DEI CAVALIERI DI MALTA

THE HEIRS TO THE TEMPLARS

The eight-pointed Maltese cross: once you've noticed it, you will see it everywhere in Rome. In most cases it is on a red flag, waving in the wind—for example, near Trajan's Markets. It is the coat of arms of one of the oldest orders of knighthood still in existence, reminiscent of the times of the Crusades and organized when Western European states came to assist the Byzantines in their fight against the Turks. The Knights of Malta (officially called the Sovereign Military Hospital Order of Saint John of Jerusalem, of Rhodes and of Malta) were not originally from Malta but from Jerusalem, where they took care of pilgrims and Crusaders in a pilgrim hospital in the Middle Ages. Traditionally, the hospital was run by Benedictine monks, but in 1113, the hospital brethren broke away and started their own order, which was soon thereafter officially recognized by the Pope. Today, the Knights of Malta are still alive and kicking: there are about twelve thousand members, among them many clergymen and members of the European nobility. It is still a sovereign knightly order but without territory. Well, almost without territory—they do have a few patches in Rome.

It is nice to climb the Aventine Hill, especially in the spring. Then the sun is not as merciless as it can be in the middle of summer, and the rose garden is in full bloom—the road to the Grand Priory smells of rose petals. The Aventine Hill is bubbling with history, which goes back to the earliest days of the city, just as it does elsewhere in Rome. Here the plebeians from fifth- to third-century BCE Rome are said to have gathered on several occasions to rebel against the privileged position of the patricians. More precisely, they organized a general people's strike over and over, halting public life completely. The Italian members of parliament who famously gathered on the Aventine and spoke out against the fascist regime in 1924 had good reasons for choosing this spot for their strike.

The road to the top does not reveal anything of that history. The smell of roses makes way for the cheerful sight of orange trees in bloom in the Giardino degli Aranci, next to the beautiful Santa Sabina. The street ends on the Piazza dei Cavalieri di Malta, which at first does not show much of the Villa Malta, seat of the Grand Priory, and the adjacent Santa Maria del Priorato. The complex was built in 939 as a Benedictine cloister. Inside they created a church dedicated to Saint Basil (San Basilio). Later, villa and church on the Aventine became property of the Templars, but when their possessions were transferred to the Order of Malta in 1312, this became the seat of the Grand Priory of the Sovereign Military Order of Malta. By now, their assets had grown exponentially, both in Asia Minor and in Europe: the inheritance of the Templars was an enormous complement to the many donations they had received from grateful Crusaders in the course of the centuries. To oversee all those possessions in each area, they established a Grand Priory, each of which in turn was divided into commanderies. Today, the Grand Master, who dons a black robe, is still in charge of these.

In 1530, the island of Malta was added to the list of possessions. Charles V gave the island to the order of the knighthood. It turned out to be a gift with some ancillary issues: the Knights of Malta had to defend their recently obtained territory soon afterward against Turkish invasions. Eventually the name stuck, but not the possession. Napoleon rejected orders of knighthood and did not recognize the claim the order made on the island. Furthermore, in 1800, Malta was seized by Great Britain. From this moment onward, the Order of Malta has been a sovereign state in name only. The knights moved their seat, successively, to Saint Petersburg, Catania, and Ferrara, but they eventually found a permanent base in Rome, where they have enjoyed recognition and protection from the Holy See ever since.

When Cardinal Benedict Pamphili became Grand Master of the Order of Malta, they were working on the Aventine Grand Priory and the square in front of it. In 1765, Pope Clement XIII (also a member of the order) commissioned his nephew, Giovanni Battista Piranesi, to come up with a new design for the square and for the facade of the San Basilio, which on the occasion of the dedication was renamed Santa Maria del Priorato. An inscription flanked by two small obelisks still commemorates this. In the church itself you will find Piranesi's tomb. Legend has it that Piranesi was a secret admirer of the Order of Malta, which is why he hid a series of hints, codes, and symbols in his square. There is said to be a hidden holy Templars ship, which has been ready for centuries to be launched at some point and set sail for the Holy Land. The Aventine Hill as a whole is a symbol of that crusader ship: the southern part, which descends to the Tiber, has the shape of an enormous "v" and represents the bow. The entrance gate of the Villa Malta is the rear deck, and the labyrinths in the gardens symbolize the mish-mash of rigging. The "forest" of obelisks on the square itself represents the trees (logs) that will be needed to launch the ship. Upon closer inspection you will find all sorts of strange symbols carved into those obelisks—secret messages, which, supposedly, only "insiders" can read.

Through the keyhole of the (always closed) entrance gate of the Villa Malta, behind which the Grand Priory of the centuries-old Order of Malta is concealed, we are allowed only a very small glimpse. Together with a *palazzo* on the Via dei Condotti, this villa represents the only territory of the sovereign order. Peeping through the keyhole, you will not only have a perfect panoramic view of the dome of Saint Peter's, but you will also see—just like in Vatican City—a strip of non-Italian territory.

XXIV

VIA COLA DI RIENZO

ROME WITHOUT POPES

Everything, even the exact location of a statue, can be very significant in Rome. Some statues indicate a long-gone temple, such as Madama Lucrezia and the marble foot in the Via del Piè di Marmo; others were misidentified for centuries and mistakenly given a prominent spot, like Marcus Aurelius on the Capitoline. And then there are the crime-scene sculptures, marking the spot where someone's life violently ended. The most well-known example of this is the statue of philosopher Giordano Bruno, on the spot where he was burned at the stake on the Campo de' Fiori. Cola di Rienzo got such a statue, too. He was dragged by his hair from the tall steps of the Church of Santa Maria in Aracoeli and hanged down below as a trophy of the people. But this was to no avail: the daily flow of tourists passes by without noticing him.

We discover this forgotten page of Rome's history in a different part of the city: on the street that leads from the Villa Borghese to the Vatican. In addition to his own statue in Rome, at the foot of the Church of Santa Maria in Aracoeli, Cola di Rienzo also has a perfectly straight shopping street named after him. It is the irony of fate that the link between the Vatican and the Villa Borghese, between pope and nobility, was named after this man, whose full name was Nicola di Rienzo Gabrini.

Cola di Rienzo, born in 1313, was a child of his time. Of course, pilgrims and popes had left their mark on the course of the city's history in Late Antiquity and the early Middle Ages, but many other movements and developments were happening simultaneously. For example, in the twelfth century, it became clear that, in addition to the Pope and families of nobility, which traditionally had a claim to power, another powerful group was slowly emerging from the working class: the bourgeoisie. As was the case in the rest of Europe, practitioners of the same trade (merchants, bankers, craftsmen) were organized into guilds, and together they appeared stronger than they had been individually. In the mid-twelfth century, the Vatican even allowed the united Roman citizens to form their own senate—although the senators still had to be appointed by the Pope, preserving his ultimate authority. Nevertheless, the representative body of Roman citizenry (the *comune*) held its own assemblies and trials, choosing the Capitoline as its home. The city government of Rome still resides there.

The indulgent attitude of the Vatican toward the new citizenry must have been a matter of "picking your battles." The Pope was most happy when the Roman citizenry kept quiet—he had enough to deal with, like several European monarchs competing for and claiming the secular power in Rome. When Pope Clement V made a radical decision in 1309 to move the Holy See to Avignon in France, it became apparent that the attacks by those monarchs had seriously and negatively affected the situation in Rome. There the Pope could at least count on the protection of his French family, and he found peace and security. For seventy years, the popes resided in Avignon, a period known in history as the "Babylonian Captivity of the Papacy."

That situation had an impact on Rome: with the papal authority far away in France, unrest and chaos reigned in the city. Rome's reputation worsened, and pilgrims avoided it, ending the economic stimulus provided by pilgrimage and accelerating the city's decline. The combination of absent authority and declining prosperity was disastrous. In that troubled Rome, Cola di Rienzo grew up as the son of an innkeeper and a laundress. When he was old enough to be concerned about the situation in Rome, he voiced fierce criticism about it on several occasions. What had happened to the great, proud Rome of yesteryear? How could they live in this mess? More and more citizens of Rome listened to di Rienzo. He was eloquent and appeared very convincing and charismatic, so much so that he called on the citizens of Rome to establish a *buono stato*—a good, decent state—in 1347, when he was not yet thirty-five. On the Capitoline, home of the *comune*, Cola di Rienzo proclaimed the founding of this New State. The promise was simple: law and order would return to the streets of Rome.

To mark the beginning of the New State, Cola di Rienzo literally started a new era; he proclaimed year one of the Liberated Republic. After all, Rome had been "liberated" by him from criminals and robbers, who had been in charge for too long. With improved security, the pilgrims slowly returned to the holy places of the city, and merchants dared to display their wares again. This success caused Cola di Rienzo's ideals to grow beyond Rome; his biggest wish was to unite Italy and make Rome its proud capital. With the papacy far away in France, nobody was stopping him from inviting all the Italian princes to Rome and being greeted as the Roman leader. In the eyes of Cola di Rienzo, the New Italy was an indisputable fact. But the more he felt like a monarch, the more he behaved like one. He had an ever-expanding entourage and wanted to have his own army; he overspent and needed taxes to pay for everything. Criticism about the exorbitant expenses grew. The grumbling in the streets evolved into a people's rebellion, and Cola di Rienzo was expelled.

Only years later, in 1354, did Cola di Rienzo dare return to Rome. He entered the city as an envoy of Pope Innocent VI, and Rome gave him a second chance. Again he restored order. But the many taxes he levied on salt and wine enraged the people again. Cola di Rienzo was blamed for everything that had gone wrong. At the bottom of the Capitoline Hill, a furious mob demanded his life on October 8, 1354. Cola di Rienzo tried unsuccessfully to evade the crowd. The man with grand dreams for Rome was beaten by a group of citizens and reportedly torn limb from limb. Cola di Rienzo, or whatever was left of him, was dragged from the highest steps of the Church of Santa Maria in Aracoeli and hanged by his feet as a trophy of the people. You can still find his statue on that spot.

When Gregory XI (1370–1378) ended the self-imposed exile of the popes and returned to Rome, he made a decision that had serious consequences for the Rome of today—he chose permanently to substitute the Patriarchate of Laterans with the Vatican living and working quarters. Every pope since then who has received the keys to St. Peter's has followed his example.

XXV

VIA DEL CORSO

THE VENETIAN POPE AND CARNIVAL

Slowly but surely, we start to walk into the Rome of the Renaissance. The word *Renaissance* may bring to mind a city full of grand art, linked to even grander names like Michelangelo and Raphael, but those images would be misleading. In the early fifteenth century, Rome did not look anything like Florence or Venice, with their cosmopolitan elites making their fortunes on the international market. Following the demise of Cola's short-lived republic, feudal nobility again dominated Rome, with well-known family names such as Colonna and Orsini. Their private armies and local power base were reminiscent of their medieval predecessors. The city had lost most of its splendor and looked much the way it had in the Middle Ages. Urban development was mainly clustered around the places of pilgrimage, but large parts of the city were used as vineyards or simply consisted of overgrown gardens and ruins. The Campo Vaccino, a "field of cows," had replaced the Forum Romanum. The infamous Tarpeian Rock on the Capitoline Hill had also become a grazing meadow, and it was now referred to as the Mons Caprinus, "Goat Mountain."

The Via del Corso, today Rome's "Fifth Avenue," did not exist yet. In antiquity, the Via Flaminia began at the foot of the Capitoline Hill, just west of Trajan's Markets. That street, the foundation of the later Corso, ran north, in the direction of the Ponte Milvio. The current-day Via del Corso, however, ends after a mile, on the Piazza del Popolo. In antiquity, the Campus Martius, one of the most densely built parts of the city outside the old center, lay west of the

Via Flaminia. Both in Late Antiquity and in the Middle Ages, people lived and worked around the Via Flaminia. The street then became known simply as "the wide road," Via Lata. Slowly this Via Lata was frequented less and less. People preferred circumventing it, via the current-day Via Biberatica and the Piazza San Silvestro. That alternative route to the north of the city was not faster, but it was drier.

For Rome, the Tiber has always been a blessing and a curse. The papal chronicles report the numerous times the river left its bed to cover the city plains. Since Rome's earliest history, the city's squares and streets were regularly inundated—severe flooding occurred at least once every fifty years, but often more frequently. The Via Lata lay in the middle of the area that was most often flooded. As Pope Paul II (1464–1471), Pietro Barbo decided that this situation was no longer tenable. In 1467, he fixed the Via Lata so that most of it ran exactly parallel to the old Via Flaminia again. Earlier, when he was a cardinal, he had built a city palace for himself at the beginning of the street. Since Pietro Barbo was a Venetian by birth, he called it Palazzo Venezia. Today's Piazza Venezia was indirectly named after it.

Cardinals building city palaces was a trend that spread farther and farther throughout the city, helping shape the renaissance of Rome. At first this claim might seem an exaggeration, but the papal administrative apparatus, the Curia, had grown exponentially since its return from exile in Avignon. It performed more and more administrative, legal, and financial functions. By the sixteenth century, the entire apparatus, including executive officers and papal staff, consisted of around two thousand people. The College of Cardinals also grew steadily and became more and more cosmopolitan. Families of nobility from all over Italy supplied cardinals, like the famous House of Medici from Florence or the Venetian Pietro Barbo. Although the Christian faith propagated frugality, the standard for cardinals became ostentatious splendor and magnificence. Since Pope Nicholas V had claimed, in the mid-fifteenth century, that the common people could only understand the grandeur of the Church through magnificent architecture, ostentation was increasingly permitted in religious circles. All elected cardinals from outside the city built a suitable residence in Rome, suitable in terms of their appearance but also of space. On average, each cardinal brought in a family and an entourage of nearly a hundred people. Pietro Barbo's Palazzo Venezia was only the beginning—under Sixtus VI, the College of Cardinals was extended to about thirty members.

Barbo became Pope, so he stayed in Rome awhile longer. He must have missed his native city because he not only named his palazzo after it, but as Pope Paul II, he also began to organize Venetian customs such as carnival on his doorstep. Romans already celebrated this festival, of course, but that was mostly on and around the Monte Testaccio, just outside the city. Paul II turned it into a grand and centrally organized carnival and added elements like masquerades and public banquets. The most spectacular part of the carnival festivities, also expanded by Paul II, were the races (*corse*) held on Shrove Tuesday. They called these horse races Corse dei Bàrberi, after the berbero, a North African horse breed. The reared, wild horses hurtled riderless through the former Via Lata, which from then on was called the Via del Corso. Horse races and tournaments in honor of carnival were organized in other parts of the city, too; for example, from the Campo de' Fiori across the Ponte Sant'Angelo (Bridge of Angels) to St. Peter's Basilica. The famous Borgia Pope Alexander VI even added an infamous prostitute race to the colorful palette of races.

The race basically ran from the Arch of Portugal (no longer there) at the level of the Via della Vite to the current-day Piazza Venezia. Pope Paul II could comfortably watch the finish line from his own palazzo. Pope Alexander VII tore down the Arch of Portugal in the seventeenth century to make way for the immensely popular horse races. The carnival festival was allowed for several centuries, until the race of 1883 resulted in a death. After this incident, the races were prohibited, but the street name Via del Corso would survive. When Italian king Umberto I died, the street name was officially changed to Corso Umberto I. In 1944, the street was temporarily given the name Corso del Popolo, but two years later the name Via del Corso returned.

XXVI

VIA DEI CORONARI

THE AWAKENING OF A RENAISSANCE CITY

At sunset, the last pilgrims left St. Peter's Basilica en masse, still enchanted by their long-awaited face-to-face with the tomb of Saint Peter. Hordes walked toward the Castel Sant'Angelo at the same time, to the only bridge that could lead them across the Tiber back into the city. It was the Holy Year 1450, and Rome could simply no longer cope with the influx of pilgrims, which had resumed since the end of the papal exile and had reached new heights in this Holy Year. When the crowd made their way across the Ponte Sant'Angelo, the bridge's railing collapsed. Countless pilgrims perished—they were trampled on or swallowed up by the Tiber.

As was the case in Late Antiquity, the incoming pilgrims were the engine behind a few urban renovations that changed Rome from an embellished medieval citadel into a respected Renaissance city. In the course of the Middle Ages, travelers came to Rome more and more often for legal reasons since the Papal Court was there, too. Cardinals' brand-new *palazzi* adorned the streets of Rome, but the streets themselves—and the entire urban design—were in need of renovation, especially where they had been trodden daily by pilgrims. The area west of the Piazza Navona (Via dei Coronari, Via Giulia, Via dei Banchi Nuovi) was reshaped, more or less on behalf of those pilgrims, so we might consider it the "Renaissance quarter." The streets in this part of the city, between the city center and the Vatican, had not only become logistical arteries for pilgrimages, but they were also prime spots for popes to leave their mark for believers from all over the world, just as the cardinals had envisioned they would do with their impressive *palazzi*. For example, the popes attached their names to those urban renewal projects, like Sixtus IV with the Ponte Sisto, the bridge that was to provide an alternative route to St. Peter's Basilica—a direct reaction to the drama of 1450.

That same Pope Sixtus IV, born Francesco Della Rovere, opened the Via dei Coronari—today a street frequented by shoppers for antiques and fashion clothing. In antiquity, this street, which runs from the top of the Piazza Navona toward the Tiber, was known as the Via Recta. The Piazza Navona did not exist yet then, but the Stadium of Domitian did. In the Middle Ages, the Via Recta became the Via di Tor Sanguigna, named after a nearby tower. Sixtus IV jumped on the opportunity to renovate this straight street, down which just about every pilgrim walked. The Via di Tor Sanguigna was an important part of the pilgrims' route, which led from the Porta di Ripetta to St. Peter's Basilica. When Sixtus IV dedicated the street as the Via dei Coronari, in the fifteenth century, that new name reflected its new purpose. Along the Via dei Coronari, more and more merchants gathered to sell all kinds of religious objects and images. They mainly sold rosaries to pilgrims, or *coronari del rosario*.

The Via dei Coronari gained fame in Rome, not least because of a number of flamboyant inhabitants. In the mid-fifteenth century, we find, at number 148, a certain Prospero Mochi, someone high up, with a seat in the Apostolic Camera and Commissary General of the works of fortification of Rome during Pope Paul III. He had many wise sayings carved into his house, which passersby even today can take to heart. On the door is the following inscription: *tua puta que tute facis* ("Consider all that you do"). On the second floor you will find the name of the former owner: *p. de mochis abbr.a.* (Prospero Mochi Abbreviatore Apostolico), and on the third floor the inscription *non omnia possumus omnes* ("All of us cannot do everything") and *promissis mane* ("Keep your promises").

The most famous character in Roman history, however, resided at 156 Via dei Coronari. It was the home of Fiammetta Michaelis, the most well-known courtesan of Renaissance Rome (along with Imperia, another famous woman of ill repute, who may have lived on the same street). The house on the Via dei Coronari was given to her by papal decree, when it stood empty following the death of the previous owner, Cardinal Piccolomini. She received a few other houses and a vineyard, to boot. Needless to say, Fiammetta's beauty was legendary. That is why the Romans whispered that she was the favorite prostitute of Cesare Borgia, the eldest son of Pope Alexander VI.

XXVII

VIA GIULIA

THE STREET AND CITY OF JULIUS II

In the early sixteenth century, a new pope took office who left his mark everywhere in Rome. These marks are still visible, especially in Vatican City and in the nearby "Renaissance quarter." Cardinal Giuliano Della Rovere was elected pope on October 30, 1503, and took the name Julius II. This was obviously a name close to his birth name, but he also wanted to evoke an association with Julius Caesar. Julius II intended to make Rome into a dignified metropolis, a *caput mundi*, as it had been during the time of Caesar. He did make history in all sorts of ways: as a war pope in a number of conflicts (between the Papal State and the Republic of Venice, France, and the influential Borgia family), but also as *maecenas* and patron of great artists (commissioning Michelangelo, Raphael, and others), and as the builder who had the first stone laid for the new St. Peter's Basilica. With the aid of architect Bramante, he was also responsible for creating "the most beautiful street of Rome."

Julius II was a man of many faces: on the one hand, he allegedly used his walking stick to threaten anyone he didn't like. On the other, he was a great lover of art and classics, commissioning several of Rome's masterpieces. He did not conceal his strong aversion to his predecessor, Borgia Pope Alexander VI. His disdain for Alexander VI, who was indeed infamous for his debauchery, was so great that he refused to occupy the papal apartments that Rodrigo Borgia had furnished. Julius II asked a young painter from Urbino, a fellow townsman of his main architect Bramante, to decorate some other rooms for him. These new papal apartments in the Vatican would become world famous under the name of that painter: the Stanze di Raffaello, or the Raphael Rooms. But that is not all; at about the same time, Julius II also commissioned Michelangelo to paint the ceiling of the chapel that his uncle, Pope Sixtus IV Della Rovere, had built and named after himself: the Sistine Chapel.

Initially, Michelangelo did not like the assignment. He had just finished the *David* statue, and if anything, its success proved that he was better with the chisel than with the paintbrush. Michelangelo was a sculptor—and a really good one. Moreover, he had been summoned to Rome for an entirely different assignment, designing a tomb for Julius II. He had set his mind to that task and had even already ordered the necessary materials to be sent to Rome. Bramante, who did not really get along well with Michelangelo, reportedly abused his position by personally convincing the Pope to remove Michelangelo from the tomb project. Instead, Bramante advised the Pope to ask Michelangelo to paint the ceiling of the Sistine Chapel. Bramante expected Michelangelo to refuse that commission, which would result in Julius II no longer giving him work. Imagining the improbable scenario in which Michelangelo, who did not have much experience as a painter, would accept the commission; Bramante was sure that Michelangelo would not be as good as Raphael, and so the end result was doomed to be of inferior quality.

When Michelangelo showed Julius II that final result, on October 31, 1512, the Pope and all the cardinals agreed that if Raphael was the master of beauty, then Michelangelo had just achieved the sublime. Even Raphael himself, Michelangelo's archrival, was very impressed. Raphael was so impressed that he decided to make last-minute adjustments to his design for the *School of Athens*, in the *stanze* next to the Sistine Chapel, on which he had been working since the fall of 1508. The *School of Athens* was a tribute to several artists, disguised as Greek philosophers. In the original sketches, which have survived, the figure to the left in the foreground is missing: an artistic, bearded man who is visibly reluctant to be attending the philosophy course. By adding that figure, Raphael gave Michelangelo his place in this masterpiece, in the shape of Heraclitus. Meanwhile, Bramante must have wished he had not whispered so much into the Pope's ear.

As an architect, Bramante himself had acquired such a reputation under Pope Alexander VI Borgia that Julius II accepted him into his inner circle, in spite of Bramante's intimate relationship with the Borgias. Bramante had proven, with the *tempietto* in the San Pietro in Montorio, that he could emulate classical architectural ideals without sacrificing contemporary principles, and this must have attracted the attention of the new, classics-loving Pope. The round temple has been known ever since as the prototype of Renaissance architecture.

In the meantime, ordinary Romans were not too happy with Julius II. Rumor had it that Julius mainly spent his time in "vineyards of the Lord," and they gave the Pope's favorite architect the not-so-flattering nickname *maestro ruinante* ("master destroyer"). Bramante owed this to the fact that Julius II had made him the chief architect of the construction projects of the new St. Peter's Basilica and of the Cortile Belvedere (a large courtyard for Julius' art collection, between the *casino del belvedere* of Pope Innocent VIII and the rest of the Vatican—which would later become the Vatican Museums).

As far as the construction of the new St. Peter's Basilica in 1506 goes, Bramante did not get to experience much more than the ceremony surrounding the laying of the first stone. Following his death, a satire was published that is indicative of the reputation that Bramante had acquired in Rome. In the story, written by Guarna da Salerno in 1516, Bramante appears before Saint Peter at the Pearly Gates. Saint Peter admonishes him for having wanted to demolish St. Peter's Basilica on Earth, prompting Bramante to complain about the bad condition of the road he has just traveled on from Earth to Heaven. He proposes building a pretty spiral staircase (a reference to the *chiocciola*, the "snail stairs" he designed for the Vatican) and tackling the entire Paradise while he is at it—it is about time Saint Peter gets a decent home. The twist at the end of the story is the best: Saint Peter decides that Bramante must wait at the Gates until the new St. Peter's Basilica is finished.

Needless to say, it took quite awhile to finish the new basilica. In the streets of Rome the new St. Peter's Basilica must have been a project like Boston's Big Dig, the Chunnel, and the metro expansion in Amsterdam: a construction project that got out of hand, while powerless inhabitants of the city could only shake their heads in dismay. One of the reasons it took so long is that many artists and architects got involved after Bramante's death. Eventually, Michelangelo let go of his personal disdain for Bramante, which he had never concealed, and used Bramante's design as a source of inspiration for his plans for St. Peter's Basilica, which he presented in 1546. The drawings show the Basilica as we marvel at it today, including the giant dome. The construction project was so grand that it outlived Michelangelo and was modified on several occasions. It was not until 1626 that Pope Urban VIII consecrated the new St. Peter's Basilica.

Apparently, Julius largely ignored the *communis opinion* as pope. He continued his construction plans, both in the Vatican and in the center of Rome. In the city, he launched a large urban development project, consisting of the construction of several roads. The connection between the Vatican and the Ponte Sisto (his uncle Sixtus IV's bridge) was to become the most extraordinary of these roads, and for this, Julius had again contracted his favorite engineer and architect, Bramante. It was designed as a straight, one-kilometer road, parallel to the Tiber, the straightest, tidiest, and longest street that had been constructed in centuries. Its name was Via Giulia, "Julius' street." Beautiful city palaces in Renaissance style were built along both sides of the Via Giulia, and soon this kilometer was known as "the most beautiful street of Rome." The Via Giulia has long kept that reputation, in part because in a later stage all sorts of luxury stores and galleries were opened there.

The Via Giulia remained a rich neighborhood for a long time. Despite its Renaissance grandeur, the street also housed a symbol of poverty: the Santa Maria dell'Orazione e Morte church. Beginning in 1573, this church looked after Rome's anonymous dead, the nameless bodies that people found in the street, in the ditch, or in the Tiber in earlier times. The skulls and bones of those paupers were namelessly laid to rest in the crypt. The brethren wanted to implore each visitor: *memento mori*, "remember that you have to die." Or, as is somewhat more bluntly stated on the facade: *hodie mihi cras tibi*—"My turn today, yours tomorrow." Between 1552 and 1896, more than eight thousand bodies were laid to rest in the underground grave site, so that literally everything you can see in the crypt today—including the decorations and the lamps—is made of skulls and bones.

Outside the church, you can see an arch over the Via Giulia. It is a symbol of the architectural optimism—or of the hubris—of the High Renaissance. Here Michelangelo had wanted to build a floating bridge that would connect the Palazzo Farnese and the Villa Farnesina—spanning the Tiber. The project was never completed, but the first step is still visible from above the Via Giulia.

XXVIII

PIAZZA DEL CAMPIDOGLIO

A SQUARE REBORN

On December 14, 1471, barely four months after he was elected pope, Sixtus IV made an extraordinary decision. He wanted to donate his private collection of masterpieces from antiquity to the people of Rome. So he gave custody of the collection to the Roman Senate, which had resided on the Capitoline Hill since the Middle Ages. The generous donation included a group of famous bronze statues that had stood in the Lateran Palace until then, among which was the *Lupa* ("She-wolf") and the *Spinario* ("Boy with thorn"). Together with other ancient works of art (like the colossal hand and the head of a statue of Constantine), they were housed in the Palazzo dei Conservatori, one of the two administrative buildings on the Capitoline Hill. Now, in accordance with the wishes of Sixtus IV, not only high-ranking clergymen but also ordinary Roman citizens would be able to enjoy these centuries-old masterpieces up close. This is how the Capitoline Museums got their start, making them some of the oldest museums in the world.

The Renaissance, originating in Florence but quickly expanding to Rome, resulted in several changes to the Vatican's appearance and the city's pilgrim-related surroundings. But the new artistic ideals of harmony and symmetry, inspired by the art, architecture, and literature from antiquity, were not only applied to places where the papal powers were evident; the hill of the administrative division, the *comune*, and the Capitoline Hill also underwent a transformation. The Capitoline Hill, the sometime home of the great temple of Jupiter Optimus Maximus, a proud symbol of the unlimited power of Rome, was a far cry from what it once was. Not much more could be found on the "Monte Caprino" than the two administrative buildings of the city in the midst of overgrown ruins, grazing cattle, and an occasional market.

In 1536, nine years after his troops pillaged Rome, raping and humiliating its inhabitants to the core (the Sacco di Roma, during which De' Medici Pope Clement VII and his court fled via the Passetto di Borgo to the Castel Sant'Angelo), the Roman-German Emperor Charles V planned a visit to the city, which he regarded as the capital of his Holy Roman Empire. It was supposed to be a triumphal parade to the Capitoline Hill, like those of the successful generals of the Roman Republic. Paul III, Pope since 1534, must have scratched his head at seeing the Capitoline Hill turned into "Goat Mountain." In order to avoid Charles V getting stuck in the mud when he dismounted from his horse, Paul III decided that the hill needed a square. It was almost natural that the job would be assigned to Michelangelo.

The oval square that still adorns the top of the Capitoline Hill today originated on Michelangelo's drawing table. Paul III basically gave Michelangelo carte blanche—although he was told to integrate the existing administrative buildings into his design, including a bronze equestrian statue, which the Pope had moved from the Lateran Palace to the Capitoline Hill just before Michelangelo started his work. The equestrian statue of Emperor Marcus Aurelius, which had survived the Middle Ages simply because the people thought it represented the first Christian emperor, Constantine, instead of the heathen emperor-philosopher Marcus Aurelius, was to have a prominent spot and a fitting shelf in the middle of the new square. In 1990, the statue was moved back inside; a copy now stands on the square.

Michelangelo designed two of the three buildings that today still encircle the Piazza del Campidoglio: the Palazzo Senatorio and the Palazzo dei Conservatori. That is to say, he designed their new facades and added the steps to the

Senatorial Palace. The Palazzo Nuovo, which together with the Palazzo dei Conservatori forms the Capitoline Museums today, wasn't built until the seventeenth century. Michelangelo designed a geometrically perfect pavement for the square (which wasn't actually installed until 1940), and he decorated the entire square with classical statues that had ties to the city of Rome. At the top of the monumental steps leading up the hill (the *cordonata*), we find statues of the Dioscuri, Castor and Pollux. The goddess Roma, a statue that was placed there only after Michelangelo's modifications, stands behind Marcus Aurelius, but so do Michelangelo's river gods (the Nile and the Tigris), lying on either side of Roma. The tiger symbolizing the Tigris was later changed into a she-wolf, so that the statue would from then on stand for Rome and the Tiber.

XXIX

CAMPO DE' FIORI

WHERE PEOPLE WERE BURNED AT THE STAKE

Pope Paul III leads us from the Piazza del Campidoglio down the hill, to the Campo de' Fiori, back to the days when he was still Cardinal Alessandro Farnese and had numerous houses torn down near the Campo de' Fiori to make way for the construction of his controversial Renaissance palace, the Palazzo Farnese. He had spent some time in prison and had never officially been ordained, but that did not prevent Borgia Pope Alexander VI, who had never had much trouble disregarding conventions, from including Alessandro Farnese in the College of Cardinals. It was clear to everyone to what Farnese owed this honor: all of Rome knew that his beautiful sister Giulia was the unofficial mistress of Rodrigo Borgia, Pope Alexander VI. To be exact: she was his most idolized and favorite paramour, but she was not his only one.

Rodrigo also had an "official" mistress, the woman he had been with when he himself was still a cardinal. Her name was Vannozza Cattanei, a noble lady whose family came from Mantova. She managed a few taverns and other businesses in Rome, such as the Locanda della Vacca in the Vicolo del Gallo, an alley near the Campo de' Fiori. In the Locanda, you can still find her family crest on the wall. The coat of arms carries inward-pointing lions in the upper right-hand and lower left-hand corners, crests of the Cattanei family. In the upper left-hand corner there is a bull; in the lower right-hand corner, six light and dark stripes—both crests of the Borgia family. Of course, these Borgia symbols had been added to the crest: Vannozza was not only Rodrigo Borgia's mistress but also the mother of his four children:

Cesare, Lucrezia, Juan, and Gioffre. Vannozza's Locanda della Vacca had provided her easy access to Rome's highest circles. Important men loved coming to her "tavern" because of the extensive selection of courtesans that Vannozza offered her high-ranking guests.

Toward the end of the fifteenth century, *locande* such as Vannozza's, but also taverns and eateries, were popping up like mushrooms on and around the Campo de' Fiori. The large market of Rome had been moved to the Piazza Navona in 1478, and that was clearly visible throughout the entire area. At that time, the Campo de' Fiori was just a field with poppies, daisies, and forget-me-nots amid the residential palaces of the aristocratic Orsini family. Thanks to this period, the square was never called a *piazza*: *campo de' fiori* is Italian for "field of flowers." The arrival of the market (and the never-ending flow of pilgrims) made the area into an instant center of commerce and industriousness. Today you will find a large number of wine bars, bakeries, and restaurants around the Campo de' Fiori; this was not much different in the fifteenth and sixteenth centuries. At the same time, the Campo de' Fiori was a notoriously dark place. For example, it really overflowed with people when there were executions in the middle of the square.

Several pictures from the past clearly show the gallows on the Campo de' Fiori, on the side of the Palazzo Orsini Righetti. Also, today we can still see where the stake was usually set up on the square. On June 9, 1889, a statue made by Ettore Ferrari was unveiled. It still attracts small groups of admirers. It represents philosopher Giordano Bruno, who was burned at the stake for heresy on February 17, 1600. In sixteenth-century Italy, the Roman Catholic Church still determined people's worldviews to a great extent, despite the Reformation, but Giordano Bruno had his own ideas. There is no doubt that he believed in a god, but one who was not a puppeteer directing the world from up above. According to Bruno, god was on Earth as an "inspiring principle." The thought that god is omnipresent is also known as pantheism, and Bruno was very much a pantheist. He did not believe in a personal god as depicted on the ceiling of the Sistine Chapel or in the appearance of Jesus as the Son of God. With this, he signed his own death sentence.

When Bruno heard his death sentence, he said, "Maybe you, my judges, condemn me in more fear than I am suffering as the one condemned." He was undoubtedly right—the Church had been through challenging times, and it was facing a growing group of opponents. Selling indulgences to finance the construction of the new St. Peter's Basilica by Pope Leo X had upset many. The monk Savonarola, and later Martin Luther, had denounced these and other excesses. The devastating Sacco di Roma had been painful proof of that resentment. For Bruno, this was all ancient history; in his days, the fierce ecclesiastical countermovement led by Pope Sixtus V known as the Counter-Reformation was in full swing. Bruno had to defend himself over and over again before the Inquisition; his books ended up on the *Index Librorum Prohibitorum* ("List of Prohibited Books"), and he was eventually burned at the stake.

The papal censure could not prevent Bruno from becoming a martyr of freethinkers, a symbol of his time or perhaps of the changing times. Not until several centuries later, in 1889, was his statue erected, with his gaze in the direction of St. Peter's Basilica. Erecting the statue was still controversial then, with the Vatican and the Roman city government protesting. After all, Bruno was a symbol of religious (and therefore civil) disobedience. Who wished to put that on a pedestal? This notwithstanding, a University of Rome committee had issued an international subscription to raise funds to make the statue in 1876. In 1889, one year after the election of a new city government, it was finally unveiled. The controversies were not over by then: on June 30 of that year, Pope Leo XIII, in a speech titled "Quod Nuper," called the statue a "symbol of those who opposed Catholicism."

Below Bruno's feet is an inscription in bronze: A BRUNO—IL SECOLO DA LUI DIVINATO—QUI—DOVE IL ROGO ARSE ("To Bruno—the century he predicted—here—where the fire burned"). His ideas finally resonated, but it came too late for him. Although, in 1999, Pope John Paul II apologized on behalf of the Church for the execution of Giordano Bruno, he has never officially been rehabilitated. His ideas are actually still incompatible with the official Church doctrine. In protest, showing sympathy with and admiration for Bruno, scientists still gather on the Campo de' Fiori on February 17, the anniversary of Bruno's death. They meet among the market stalls (in 1869, the market was moved from the Piazza Navona to its current location), on the spot "where the fire burned."

XXX

VIA DELLE QUATTRO FONTANE

HAPPINESS IS A STREET

There is no more appropriate street in Rome to take us into the Baroque era than Sixtus' Via delle Quattro Fontane. The "street of the four fountains" was once two miles long, running from the Trinità dei Monti (near the Spanish Steps) to the Santa Croce in Gerusalemme. It was then called Strada Felice, literally "happy street," after the Pope who built it: Sixtus V, Felice Perretti. His perfectly straight street was meant to connect the Pincio Hill with the Santa Maria Maggiore. It was just one of the many new roads that Sixtus V would build in Rome—in addition to the dozens of roads he had repaved.

Whereas famous Renaissance popes like Julius II focused on reviving the (classical) past, Sixtus V would become a great innovator (and, inevitably, destroyer) who wanted to lead Rome and the Church into the future. He brought rigorous reforms: the pilgrim churches and the hills of Rome were connected via beautiful, straight streets, and on those streets no structure jutted out dangerously anymore, thanks to a new law. Rome also became much safer: the new pope's reign of terror dealt a severe blow to major and minor criminals. The sections of the city that had been *disabitato* ("uninhabitable") for a long time now became vivacious again. From the moment he became pope in 1585, Sixtus did not lose any time carrying out his plans for the city. He tore down old Roman monuments obstructing his path without a second thought. During this time, the Colosseum barely escaped a similar fate: considering it a useless building, the Pope wanted to tear parts of it down in order to build a new road.

A man with such determination to restructure the city of Rome would not come around again after Sixtus until the twentieth century—namely, Mussolini.

After the Council of Trent, one could say this was Sixtus V's response to the Ninety-Five Theses that Martin Luther had nailed to the door of the church in 1517. Pope Leo X's indulgences racket had severely damaged the Church's reputation, but now the moment had come for the Counter-Reformation, for a reinvigorated Catholicism to celebrate its greatness and promote itself. With his renovations of the city, Sixtus V was the ideal Counter-Reformation Pope, with architect Domenico Fontana at his side. For him, Fontana rebuilt the Lateran Palace and created four fountains for the statues the Pope had placed in the busiest intersection of his Strada Felice (where today the Via del Quirinale merges into the Via XX Settembre). The first represents the River Arno, with curly hair and flanked by a lion, the symbol of Florence. A second one is the River Tiber, with an overflowing horn of plenty in his hands, and with the obligatory she-wolf. The third fountain embodies strength, represented by a well-to-do woman (or goddess) with royal symbols such as a lion and a crown. The fourth and last fountain symbolizes loyalty. It is a lady accompanied by a dog, with her arm resting on the three small heraldic mountains of Sixtus V.

You can see the Strada Felice in its entirety on a 1748 map of Rome, but it seems to have almost disappeared on an 1878 map. Indeed, the Strada Felice was slowly but surely divided into the Via Sistina, the Via delle Quattro Fontane, the Via Agostino Depretis, the Via Carlo Alberto, the Via Conte Verde, and the Via di Santa Croce in Gerusalemme. None of these street names were assigned before 1870, including the Via delle Quattro Fontane. In the early seventeenth century, this street must have been frequented by an artistic architect, whose innovative works of art not only depicted the Baroque but also the spirit of the Counter-Reformation, perhaps in this way becoming the most important defender of the faith: Gian Lorenzo Bernini. The man who followed in his shadow, on the way to a joint construction project, was Francesco Borromini. As an architect, he was at least as skilled as Bernini, but he lacked the latter's diplomatic talents and optimism.

The Palazzo Barberini, a joint construction project of Bernini and Borromini along the Via delle Quattro Fontane, was begun in 1627 by Carlo Maderno, but he died when the foundation had just been laid. In the meantime, Cardinal Maffeo Barberini had been inaugurated as Pope Urban VIII, on August 6, 1623. It would turn out to be a pivotal moment in Bernini's career. The ambitious artist was only twenty and had already made the *Rape of Proserpina* and *Apollo and Daphne*; both statues adorned (and are still adorning) the villa of Scipione Borghese, near the Porta Pinciana. Pope Urban VIII's role, mostly forced upon him, was that of a war pope (the Thirty Years' War between Catholic and Reformed states in Europe was raging), yet he also became a patron of the arts—with Bernini as his favorite protégé. When Maderno died, the Pope was happy to appoint Bernini as the new chief architect of his city palace.

Bernini had felt he needed Borromini's help at several important moments in his career, and this was one of them. In fact, Bernini was not an architect (yet), but mostly a sculptor. In addition, Borromini was a distant relative of Carlo Maderno. Bernini had worked off Borromini's designs for the bronze canopy in St. Peter's Basilica, that wonderful architectonic piece of art that Bernini also created, commissioned by Urban VIII. The two men collaborated for years on the Palazzo Barberini until its completion in 1633. The final result does not contain much of Maderno's original design. For example, the central open loggia that Maderno envisioned did not materialize. In its stead, Bernini built the Gran Salone—the large hall in which Pietro da Cortona painted frescoes.

Bernini's star rose after the Palazzo Barberini, whereas Borromini became mainly known as an eccentric and rather morbid man. Borromini nevertheless obtained his first private contract in 1634, on the Via delle Quattro Fontane. Here he was to build one of the most beautiful small churches in Rome, intersecting the four fountains: the San Carlo alle Quattro Fontane. Borromini worked on his San Carlino ("Little San Carlo") for three years. The design was a challenge: Borromini had to keep in mind that the alcove of one of the four fountains was in the intersection. That is why he designed an innovative floor map, consisting of three triangles and four ellipses pushed into one another. The elliptic centers in turn form two equilateral triangles: a great geometric construction. For the dome, Borromini crafted a fine example of optical illusion: the dome seems much higher than it is in reality. Borromini created this effect by making the pattern smaller and smaller as it went up, and by letting daylight in through invisible windows. When the San Carlo was nearing completion (Borromini did not make the facade until the end of his career), colleagues mostly denigrated and ridiculed Borromini's church. Borromini did not gain admiration until his later projects, such as the Sant'Agnese in Agone, and especially the Sant'Ivo Alla Sapienza. This did not prevent Borromini from committing suicide in 1667, having lost his battle with depression.

Up the way, on the Piazza Barberini, Bernini had worked on the widely acclaimed Triton Fountain and the so-called Fountain of the Bees, the Fontana delle Api, right behind it. It seemed as though the bees of (the coat of arms of) the Barberini were crawling across every work of art in which Bernini had a hand. Bernini's career was over when the unavoidable day came that Urban VIII died and was buried in a tomb (designed by Bernini) in St. Peter's Basilica. Fate had it that the new pope, Innocent X (Giovanni Battista Pamphili) detested his predecessor and wanted to distance himself from him in everything. The new Pope accused Urban VIII's heirs of embezzlement in 1645, one year after his death. The Holy See confiscated the Palazzo Barberini, only to return it to the family in 1653. It would then remain in possession of the Barberinis until 1949, when it was transferred from the very last heir (Sacchetti Barberini Colonna) to the Italian state.

All Bernini could do was wait for the new Pope to change his tune. Knowing that his talent couldn't be ignored, Bernini waited patiently for the moment that he would come into favor with the Pope again. Bernini kept receiving commissions, and his studio kept growing. During this period (1647–1652), he worked on a private commission: the Cornaro Chapel in the Santa Maria della Vittoria, for which he created the *Ecstasy of Saint Teresa*—nothing less than a masterpiece and a great symbol of Baroque art. Bernini's patience was rewarded; Innocent X had finally come around. Bernini's most famous Roman piece of art was commissioned by the Pamphili Pope, and in his "backyard" no less: the Piazza Navona.

XXXI

PIAZZA DELLA ROTONDA

RECYCLING IN THE PANTHEON

Before allowing ourselves to be overwhelmed by the theatrical beauty of Pamphili's Piazza Navona, we will first stop at the Piazza della Rotonda and take a moment to reflect on the dark side of Roman Baroque, in a place Bernini left behind in a tattered state. In 1625, Urban VIII gave Bernini permission to strip the Santa Maria Rotonda, better known as the Pantheon, of its bronze sheeting, so that he could construct his canopy over Saint Peter's tomb in St. Peter's Basilica. Where else would he find enough bronze to create the enormous work of art he was envisioning? After all, it was not at all unusual to find building materials in ruins and on older monuments in the city, like the temples on the Forum Romanum and the huge Colosseum.

In contrast to many other Roman monuments, the Pantheon (nicknamed *la rotonda*) had virtually been in continuous use since antiquity. In 608, the Roman temple "for all gods" was converted into a church building. Today, the Santa Maria Rotonda, officially Santa Maria ad Martyres, is still used as a church. This is incredible continuity, considering the fact that the earliest construction on the spot of the Pantheon took place between 27 and 25 BCE. At that time, Augustus' general Agrippa (63–12 BCE) paid for the construction of a temple. Excavations have brought to light remnants that indicate this must have been an "ordinary" (read: rectangular) temple, with a different orientation than the current one. Decades later, Emperor Domitian (51–96 CE) financed a number of substantial restorations of the building. These were needed because in the year 80, a fire raged in the area, damaging the temple. The most famous work done on the temple is commemorated in the still very legible inscription on the facade.

"Marcus Agrippa, the son of Lucius, made this during his third consulate," we read in translation. Indeed, Agrippa built a temple here, but that wasn't the round-shaped one. The inscription and the renovations date back to the reign of Emperor Hadrian—the work must have been done between about 118 and 125. Although most emperors very much liked to have their names chiseled into the building projects they financed, Hadrian chose not to. He much preferred to restore the honor of the very first builder, Marcus Agrippa, indirectly invoking those past glory days in the memories of the spectators.

Hadrian's renovations were considerable. He began to reuse the old temple but altered its orientation and added the rotunda. This new Pantheon, with its enormous dome, became a symbol of the ingenuity of Roman engineering. In a clever way, the architects had the full weight of the gigantic dome rest on the round-wall construction, hiding numerous arches. The distance from the floor to the top of the dome is exactly the same as the diameter of the dome. The only light penetrating the space comes from the *oculus*, the round opening in the ceiling. A long time ago, the alcoves contained the statues of all the gods of the Roman divine realm (the *pantheon*). Later those alcoves served as tombs for illustrious people from Roman and Italian history. For example, in 1520, Raphael found his final resting place there, with a few beautiful lines of poetry: "Here lies Raphael. While he lived, Mother Nature feared he would outdo her; at his death, she feared that she herself would die."

On the square in front of it, the Piazza della Rotonda, you can still find plenty of references to the colorful past of this spot in the heart of Rome. Near house number 14, there is an inscription about the market that was held here until 1847. Since the Middle Ages, meat, fish, vegetables, and fruit were sold on the Piazza della Rotonda. The mess the merchants left behind created suboptimal hygienic conditions on the square. When some stalls and shops started moving all the way into the narthex of the Pantheon, the Piazza della Rotonda became an eyesore for many popes. Yet it took until 1823 before Pope Pius VII ordered the filthy, dilapidated warehouse rooms (for the merchandise) removed. He also had the Piazza della Rotonda tiled. More than twenty years later, in 1847, the grimy market was banned from the square for good.

The fountain in the middle of the Piazza della Rotonda has been there since the fifteenth century, when Pope Eugene XV decided to add two small basins adorned with lions. Since then, the fountain has been torn down and rebuilt several times. Pope Clement XI gave the base of the fountain five steps on one side and two on the other—the fairly literal accumulation of layers of history created different levels in the square over the course of time. This same Clement also added the obelisk on top of the fountain. The obelisk was found near the Santa Maria sopra Minerva church, and it spent some time near the San Macuto church. That is why the more than twenty-foot-tall obelisk is (still) known as Il Macuteo. It is likely that this obelisk originally belonged to the Temple of the Sun in Heliopolis, in ancient Egypt. As was customary, the obelisk was gifted to the city of Rome during the Imperial Era and placed in its Isis temple.

At house number 68, we find a plaque with a strange inscription, describing a wooden floor for the Pantheon. This text refers to a special present that the city of Rome received during a 1906 visit by the mayor of Buenos Aires. The mayor was deeply impressed by the Pantheon and by the burial monuments inside it. There was one thing he did not understand, however: how could a basilica with such a history and such important tombs be located amidst so much working-class bustle? He thought the tombs deserved "to be shrouded in solemn silence." Therefore, he gave Rome a new floor for the Piazza della Rotonda, made of wood from the Argentinian rainforest, so that the eternal rest of the illustrious dead would no longer be disturbed by street noises. The wooden floor lay briefly in front of the Pantheon before it had to be removed.

Before we get too far ahead of ourselves in the history, we will return to Bernini via the bronze of the Pantheon. The old temple turned out to be a nearly endless source of materials. When Bernini had enough for his canopy, there was still enough bronze left over for the Pope to make new cannons for the Castel Sant'Angelo. A few years later, in 1632, Urban VIII commissioned Bernini to place two small campaniles on either side of the Pantheon. But from the moment they were installed, the *orecchie d'asino* ("donkey ears") were ridiculed, so they were removed in 1883.

The Romans characterized the way the Barberini Pope in particular treated the cultural heritage of the city as barbaric, an indirect reference to the havoc wreaked in Rome by the barbaric tribes when the Roman Empire fell. Pasquino, the sharp tongue of Rome, put it even more aptly: *Quod non fecerunt barbari fecerunt barberini*—"What the barbarians did not do was done by the Barberini." This is just one of the many clever, satirical puns that Pasquino and five like-minded spirits left behind. You may wonder who this eloquent, loose-lipped Roman was, who openly voiced unfettered criticism about papal policies, and, more importantly, how he got away with it.

XXXII

VIA DEL BABUINO

WHEN THE STONES TALK

One day, sometime in the fifteenth century, Pasquino, a stone statue in Rome, started to talk. It was the first among a strange group of speaking statues of Rome, the "Congregation of the Wits" (*Congresso degli Arguti*), consisting of six members with at least one thing in common nowadays: they are all in pretty bad shape. In addition to leader Pasquino, on the square by the same name, there is the earlier mentioned Madama Lucrezia on the Piazza San Marco, Marforio in the Palazzo Nuovo (Capitoline Museums), Abate Luigi on the Piazza Vidoni, Il Facchino in the Via Lata, and Il Babuino in the street named after him, the Via del Babuino. Their "speaking" consisted of commenting on the papal policies in Rome: political commentaries and straight-out criticisms were wrapped in witty verse; satire and wordplay were pasted onto the statues. There were even dialogues between the talking statues.

Although Pasquino and Marforio are the group's most well-known members, the "baboon," Il Babuino, had worthy contributions, too. The current, very straight Via del Babuino (between the Piazza del Popolo and the Spanish Steps) replaced a much less organized fifteenth-century path. The street was split. The first part was called Via dell' Orto di Napoli, since it was home to a small colony of immigrants from Naples. The second part had a somewhat sinister name. The Via del Cavalletto was not a reference to an easel (*cavalletto*) but to the method of torture that was carried out here by order of the Pope. Convicted criminals had to straddle a kind of wooden "horse." Hung from their legs were weights as heavy as the crime they had committed.

When Clement VII connected the two streets in 1525, he proudly attached his name to the new street: Via Clementina. To build a fountain, Pius V later redirected some waterways toward the Via Clementina, which was then called Via Paolina. He had an old Roman basin brought over, and above it he put an antique statue of a *silenus*—a fabulous creature from ancient Greek mythology. These creatures were associated with water sources and depicted as ugly, chubby, hairy beings, often dressed in sheepskin. In that sense, the statue of the *silenus* was true to nature: quite horrible and disheveled. The Romans considered this statue so ugly that they could only compare it to a monkey. It became popularly known as Il Babuino—the baboon.

Thanks to the many jokes and satirical remarks, the statue became more and more well known. When Il Babuino's fame was at its peak, the Romans started the *babuinate* (after the *pasquinate*, as Pasquino's satires had become known): short, anonymous, sharply formulated political slogans and satires, left behind on the statue in notes and pamphlets. They were often directly addressed to the Pope. Soon Il Babuino was rightfully admitted to the *Congresso degli Arguti*.

That Rome had fully embraced the ugly baboon was evident when persistent statements of support and protests led to it being reunited with its old Roman water basin in the original place in the Via del Babuino in 1957. When the *palazzo* of Alessandro Grandi, against which the fountain was built, was torn down in 1738 to make way for the Palazzo Boncompagni Cerasi, the combination was moved to an inlet down the street. Then, in 1887, the Babuino (Silenus) Fountain had to be relocated for practical reasons. Only the statue was moved to the courtyard of the Palazzo Boncompagni Cerasi. The old Roman basin was moved to a different fountain, in the Via Flaminia. Since 1957, however, the statue has been back in its original spot.

XXXIII

PIAZZA NAVONA

THEATER OF ROMAN STREETLIFE

Early in the morning, illustrators and other artists gather in the middle of the square. They will spend the day drawing caricatures of tourists or creating Impressionist paintings of doors and balconies, works that can be acquired for a substantial fee. The easels and street artists are surrounded by outdoor cafés where tourists pay an arm and a leg for their cappuccinos. The tourists, the street artists, the passersby—all watch the epic battle between the two artistic grand masters of the Piazza Navona: Bernini and Borromini.

In 1647 Innocent X decided that the glorified "trough for animals," as he used to call the fountain on the Piazza Navona, would be replaced by a proper successor. Girolamo Rainaldi was revamping the square already, trying to turn the Palazzo Pamphili into a city palace worthy of Innocent's papacy, which had recently begun. The Piazza Navona, a bustling square of merchants and strolling city dwellers in Baroque Rome, was therefore, in a sense, the Pope's backyard. He organized a competition for a fitting fountain among the best artists. All artists of repute were invited to submit a design sketch. That is, all but Bernini. It cost Bernini dearly that he used to be Barberini Pope Urban VIII's favorite. Borromini did participate, and he submitted a proposal for a fountain with four rivers. Encouraged by a good friend with connections in the papal court, Bernini also made a design sketch. His friend submitted Bernini's scale model. So Innocent X unknowingly saw Bernini's submission. He openly conceded that it was no contest: Bernini's design—including the four rivers he had copied from Borromini—was by far the best. In 1651, construction of the fountain started.

Bernini led the project, but he was barely involved in its actual implementation. Although following his design and aided by his artistic and technical knowhow, different artists made the four gigantic figures in the fountain. The figures symbolize the largest rivers that were known at that time: the Ganges, the Danube, the Nile, and the Rio de la Plata. Innocent X himself discovered the enormous obelisk, on April 27, 1647, on a visit to the San Sebastiano church. It was lying unattended on the ground in the archaeological zone of the Circus of Maxentius. The inscriptions on the obelisk mentioned Emperor Domitian, which made people assume that it had originally belonged to his stadium, underneath the Piazza Navona. That is why the obelisk was put on top of the Fontana dei Quattro Fiumi, where it has been since August 12, 1649.

A popular legend has it that the Fountain of the Four Rivers contains several secret clues hiding Bernini's disdain for the Sant'Agnese in Agone church on the opposite side of the square—the church that the Pope commissioned Borromini to renovate. The veil of the Nile, and the posture of the Rio de la Plata figure, seem to suggest that the river gods do not even want to look at the church. One may even see a fearful, defensive aspect to the Rio de la Plata figure—as if the marble statue is afraid the church will collapse. No matter how much we love to believe this legend today, it is impossible that Bernini purposely included these hidden clues in his fountain. The construction of the church was not begun until after the Fountain of the Four Rivers had been completed.

The very first church on the spot of the Sant'Agnese in Agone was reportedly built in 304, dedicated to Agnese, an ill-fated but pious girl who fell victim to rape at an early age. The location of the church marks the spot where she was abused; she had refused to marry a prominent Roman citizen due to her voluntary "marriage to Christ." While the torturers were tearing her clothes off, Agnese's hair began to grow miraculously, so that it covered her entire body. The man who had tried to take her virginity dropped dead at her feet. Eventually, Agnese was killed; the Romans cut her throat with a sword. The addition of *agone* is not in reference to the pain Agnese had to endure but to the Circus Agonalis that lies twenty feet below the current square. The sporting events that were held in this ancient Stadium of Domitian were called *agones*. The square's current name is directly linked to it, roughly like this: *in agone* became *innagone*, which turned into *navone*. Piazza Navona was born.

The two other fountains on the Piazza Navona generally receive less attention. They are not as large or as impressive, and less is "happening" in them. Yet both fountains are fine examples of architecture by Jacopo Della Porta (1537–1602). On the southern end of the square we find the Fountain of the Moor, with four tritons. In the middle, the Moor is struggling with a dolphin. The statue of the Moor was not part of the original design but was added by Bernini. On the northern end of the Piazza Navona we find the Neptune Fountain, for which Della Porta only designed the basin. The statues were not added until 1878.

There is no doubt that Pamphili Pope Innocent X spruced up the Piazza Navona to improve both his public perception and his view. It is also hardly fathomable how welcome (and necessary) fountains were in an era in which clean drinking water from the tap was not available in every household. The sixteenth-century renovation of the ancient Aqua Virgo—the conduit to the city for fresh water from the sources in the hills surrounding Rome—offered an excellent opportunity to divert the pipes to the Piazza Navona area. Immediately thereafter, the construction of the fountains on the Piazza Navona was begun. It had housed a market since the second half of the fifteenth century. The square was also a meeting place, and it would not take long before all sorts of festivities and processions were taking place on the Piazza Navona. Several paintings show how the square was sometimes filled with water on these occasions, for cooling off and the entertainment of the Romans.

XXXIV

PIAZZA SAN PIETRO

THE GIANT ARMS OF BERNINI

The artist whose name is inextricably connected with Rome more than any other was eighty-two when he died. It is said that at a very advanced age, Bernini was still busy with blocks of marble every morning at seven. He couldn't help himself—his whole life, he had done nothing but work, work, work. The continuous flow of commissions, often personal assignments from the reigning Pope, never stopped. In 1656, at 58, he received a special commission from the new Pope, Alexander VII (Fabio Chigi), who, like Maffeo Barberini, would become known as a patron of the great artists of his time. The new St. Peter's Basilica was finally completed, resulting in an increase in the number of pilgrims coming to Rome. But the city attracted still more visitors: since the Renaissance, humanists and artists had traveled to the Eternal City to admire antiquities or to examine manuscripts, and during the centuries that followed, Rome attracted students and scholars. Naturally, many of them went to see the new St. Peter's Basilica. This created the need for a large, beautiful square in front of the Basilica, where all the visitors could meet. The new square would also need to offer them a good view of the Vatican *palazzi*, from which the blessings are imparted.

St. Peter's Basilica would have been unassuming during the first centuries of its existence. It started out as an unexceptional monument on the supposed grave of Saint Peter, in the middle of a necropolis full of other graves. Initiated by the Emperor Constantine in the fourth century, a new, Romanesque basilica was built. It was a relatively ordinary church, which nevertheless stuck around for hundreds of years. The centuries-long flow of pilgrims has had its impact on the Borgo, as the area below St. Peter's Basilica has been known for centuries. Raphael's *Incendio di Borgo*, depicting the devastating fire that raged in the Borgo, shows how chaos could reign in such a packed neighborhood. The *Incendio* is one of the frescoes in the *stanza* (room) named after it, a former papal dining hall, and currently part of the Vatican Museums. In the background of the fresco, Raphael eternalized the old St. Peter's Basilica. It is one of the rare depictions of the mosaic-adorned basilica.

The new St. Peter's Basilica had been worked on for ages. It was, however, still in the middle of a busy residential area. Clearing part of that area for the creation of a large open square was one of the first commissions by Pope Alexander VII after assuming the Pontificate. Legend has it that he was so meticulous in the details of his wishes that he even told Bernini the dimensions of the square and of the colonnades. Of course, Bernini himself deserves credit for the oval design with the colonnades. Every column that he designed for the square has a diameter of at least five feet. Bernini placed no fewer than 284 on the square, complemented by 88 pillars. The square itself ended up being 260 feet wide and 220 feet long. In any case, Bernini satisfied the requirement to offer pilgrims enough room: up to 400,000 faithful can gather on the square.

After the completion of Saint Peter's Square, the colonnades soon acquired a fitting nickname: the *abbraccio berniniano*, Bernini's embrace. No fewer than four rows of massive, impressive columns embrace the Piazza San Pietro. Yet, sometimes it looks as though you only see one row of columns. Blink a few times, and you see double rows again. Bernini meant to build this optical illusion into his square. If you want to know exactly what he intended, you will have to look for two focal points in the square's pavement—between the obelisk and the fountains. In a marble circle, you find the words CENTRO DEL COLONNATO, "center of the colonnade." If you go and stand exactly on the circle and look toward the colonnades nearest to you, your eyes will be misled. You will only see one row of columns instead of the four that are there. Borromini had already used similar forms of trompe-l'oeil, for example in the dome of his San Carlino and in his famous *Prospettiva*, a visually deceptive gallery in the Palazzo Spada. Illusionistic effects gained popularity during the Baroque era. Art was, more so than during the Renaissance, intended to surprise its audience. It was not only Borromini and Bernini's art that expressed this but also paintings of that era—as can be seen on the ceiling of the Sant'Ignazio di Loyola church, to which Andrea Pozzo gave an illusionary dome in the late seventeenth century. However, one painter developed his idiosyncratic style in a different direction, causing quite a stir.

XXXV

VICOLO DEL DIVINO AMORE

CARAVAGGIO IN ROME

On May 8, 1604, a young artist signed a lease for a house on the Vicolo del Divino Amore (at the time still called the Vicolo San Biagio), an alley in the center of Rome. Michelangelo Merisi, from the northern Italian town of Caravaggio, had come to Rome as a twenty-two-year-old in 1593. His first few years in Rome, he was an apprentice of an established artist. Caravaggio, the name Michelangelo went by, slowly moved into the right circles and attracted the attention of potential clients with his unmistakable talent in early Roman paintings such as *Judith Beheading Holofernes.* Thanks to his growing network, he not only received more and more commissions, but he also found a recently renovated house for himself in 1604. An improbable number of details about this move have been preserved. This is because the nearby parish of San Nicola dei Prefetti kept very accurate records of the comings and goings in the neighborhood.

Caravaggio's first large public commission in Rome was the Contarelli Chapel in the San Luigi dei Francesi (Saint Louis of the French) church. He created three paintings with scenes from the life of Saint Matthew to adorn the chapel. You can immediately understand the numerous ways in which this young, idiosyncratic artist was innovative in his work. Instead of depicting a classical, ideal image of heroic figures, Caravaggio painted what he saw around him: real people in the real world. From rotting fruit in still lifes, to old women, dirty toes, and gentle young men—regardless of the (often religious) topic—Caravaggio gave his figures on the canvas something unvarnished and human. The drama in his works is strongly enhanced by his use of light and dark (chiaroscuro), as if he were a theater producer using spotlights to present his subjects with a natural perfection. Following the Contarelli Chapel, he was commissioned in 1600 to work on the Cerasi Chapel in the Santa Maria del Popolo church. Caravaggio had made a name for himself in Rome.

In the old archives of the San Nicola dei Prefetti parish, for the years 1604–1606, you will find more than one registered renter: in addition to Caravaggio is his apprentice, Francesco—since Caravaggio could by then afford his own helper. Caravaggio and his apprentice, in turn, joined another renter: Prudenzia Bruni. Her "situation" is described, too: she was married to Bonifacio Sinibaldi, a shoemaker and poultry merchant. On the basis of these documents, historians have established that from the San Nicola dei Prefetti church, the first *palazzo* on your right was the house that was owned by Prudenzia Bruni. The same documents registered a renovation/restoration of that building during 1601–1604. On that occasion, the available living space was split into two separate dwellings. So starting on May 8, 1604, Bruni rented out half the house to Caravaggio.

It is not hard to reconstruct exactly how Caravaggio found this house. The owner of the *palazzo* was Laerzio Cherubini, the man who had commissioned him to paint *Morte della Vergine*, currently housed in the Louvre in Paris. But we can also follow other lines: Prudenzia and her husband were acquaintances of Pietropaolo Pellegrini, the assistant of the local hairstylist, Marco. The police interrogated that assistant about a disturbance in July 1597. The report of that interrogation has survived. The boy claimed to have known Caravaggio well since 1596.

In the lease that Caravaggio signed on May 8, he stipulated in writing that he would officially be allowed to modify the structure of the rented space. Bruni agreed to it, on condition that Caravaggio would pay for the return of the space to its original state before the lease was up. I will leave it to the reader's imagination to interpret Caravaggio's request. Did he want to break open part of the ceiling to let in more light, or was he perhaps looking for possibilities to work on enormous canvasses? In any case, he must have used his house mainly as a studio—Caravaggio remained prolific during his entire time in Rome, certainly after the wealthy banker and art collector Giustiani had become his patron and regular customer (*Amor Vincit Omnia* would become the most famous fruit of this relationship). Prudenzia Bruni pops up again in the official archives when she takes her corenter to court one year later. Until late January 1605, Caravaggio had paid his rent on time, but after that he stopped abruptly, incurring quite a debt between February and July. Bruni took legal steps and was given an injunction, allowing her legally to confiscate Caravaggio's belongings.

This was not the only time Caravaggio had a run-in with the law. His notorious talent went hand in hand with an equally notorious temper. In his short life, he regularly clashed with the police. He often got in trouble in Roman taverns; on several occasions, he got into fights. It was bound to go wrong at some point: an argument in 1606 about a game of tennis (or a woman, that is not clear) escalated, and Caravaggio lethally wounded his opponent. Now the master of the chiaroscuro was outlawed and had to flee Rome. Years later, on his way back to Rome after numerous wanderings, he died penniless.

The Vicolo del Divino Amore clearly does not owe its name to its most famous inhabitant. When Caravaggio moved into his rental house, the street was named for the Santi Cecilia e Biagio church, but that church was handed over to the Confraternita del Divino Amore in the eighteenth century. Despite the scandals that Caravaggio brought with him into the alley, the street is named for the Brotherhood of Divine Love to this day.

XXXVI

PIAZZA DEL POPOLO

THE ENTRANCE HALL OF ROME

If ever a woman held a triumphal march through Rome, it had to be the remarkable Northern European ex-queen of Sweden, Christina. For centuries, travelers arriving in Rome from the north entered it on the Via Flaminia, first setting foot on Roman soil in a spot we now know as the Piazza del Popolo. The square was and is situated at the top of the Tridente, the "trident" of roads formed by the Via del Babuino, the Via del Corso, and the Via di Ripetta. It makes good sense that the Porta del Popolo is considered the grand entrance of Rome, and the Piazza del Popolo the reception hall.

From here it is still possible to see through the eyes of earlier travelers to Rome because this view of the city has remained relatively untouched over the past few centuries. Upon arrival on the Via Flaminia, the very first thing people saw was the Porta del Popolo. The exterior decorations were a project Pope Pius V had entrusted to Michelangelo. The latter, fairly old at the time, passed the assignment on to his pupil Nanni di Baccio Bigio, who finished the job between 1562 and 1565. Michelangelo took the arch's pillars from the old St. Peter's Basilica—after all, he was very familiar with the construction site of the new St. Peter's.

In 1655, Alexander VII succeeded Pamphili Pope Innocent X. Alexander was a descendant of the illustrious Chigi family of Tuscan bankers. Just like his predecessor, he gladly kept Gian Lorenzo Bernini on, the undisputed master architect of the seventeenth century. The new Pope focused primarily on the "reception hall" of the city, the Piazza del

Popolo, in addition to Saint Peter's Square. The occasion for that renovation of Rome's grand entrance was a visit by the woman from the north, the self-proclaimed convert from Sweden. Christina was ex-queen of "Sweden, the Goths and the Vandals," an unconventional, capricious, art-loving woman and a champion of the free practice of the sciences. She was not in her element in Sweden; in 1654 she officially abdicated and left her Protestant homeland incognito. For years she had expressed the desire to convert to Catholicism, which was forbidden in Sweden; Rome was her destination.

On December 23, 1655, Christina of Sweden and her court entered Rome. Alexander VII had seen to it that the reception was triumphant. The Pope wanted the prominent convert Christina to be enchanted by Rome at first sight, so he offered her an unforgettable view. Bernini embellished the inside of the Porta del Popolo and added an inscription. Straight across from the gate, on the other side of the Egyptian obelisk that Sixtus V put there in 1589, Alexander VII built churches: the Santa Maria dei Miracoli and the Santa Maria in Montesanto. The two churches, which marked the corners of the Tridente, from which the three main roads led to the heart of Rome, had to be completely identical. These so-called "twin churches" would become symbols of the Piazza del Popolo. But not everything is what it seems to be. Upon closer inspection, you will notice that they are not identical. The construction of the twin churches, in which both Bernini and Carlo Fontana had a hand, was not completed until after the death of Alexander VII.

In any case, it was an impressive reception on December 23, 1655. Christina set foot on the Piazza del Popolo, where she was overwhelmed—not only by the splendor of the square but also by the bang of a cannon fired from the Castel Sant'Angelo. What followed was an endless series of festivities in the city. The procession in the courtyard garden of the Palazzo Barberini, before the eyes of thousands of cheering spectators, is the most well known of these festivities.

Christina was given an apartment in the beautiful Palazzo Farnese. On Christmas Day, Pope Alexander VII officially baptized her. She chose to be known thereafter as Christina Alexandra Maria.

The origin of the name of the square where Christina so triumphantly entered Rome is connected to the oldest building you can find there, the Santa Maria del Popolo (on the north side). The legend of the founding of the church dates back to the eleventh century. Pope Paschal II had had enough of the many stories about Nero's evil spirit wandering around the place. In 1099, he dedicated a church there in honor of the Holy Virgin Mary, in order to expel the "demon" once and for all. It is said that the construction was entirely financed by levying taxes. Because the people themselves indirectly paid for it, the church was named Santa Maria del Popolo. In the second half of the fifteenth century, Sixtus IV ordered a thorough renovation of the old church building.

If Christina had taken the time to dismount her horse and visit the Santa Maria del Popolo, she would likely have been even more impressed by the Eternal City. Half a century before her arrival, Caravaggio painted *The Conversion of Saint Paul* and *The Crucifixion of Saint Peter* in the Cerasi Chapel—masterpieces that can still be admired in their original setting. Many visited the Santa Maria del Popolo after reading Dan Brown's *Angels and Demons*, which featured its Chigi Chapel, designed by Raphael. Unfortunately, these visitors often miss the series of frescoes by Renaissance painter Pinturicchio and the two artistic tombs by Andrea Sansovino that adorn the choir.

XXXVII

PIAZZA DI TREVI

THREE PATHS TO THE TREVI FOUNTAIN

Over twenty million gallons—that is how much water flows through the Trevi Fountain in Rome every day. This has been going on since May 22, 1762, when Pope Clement XIII officially dedicated the theatrical fountain. The enormous spectacle is one hundred feet tall and seventy feet wide, and, to complete the impressive list of statistics, about twenty thousand pounds of coins are thrown into it each year. And this is one of the smallest squares in Rome. There is no doubt that this is the most spectacular place to see the water of the Aqua Virgo, the old Roman aqueduct from 19 BCE, although most tourists gather on the Piazza di Trevi just so they can toss a coin into the water of the Trevi Fountain.

The square and the fountain were named after the intersection of three roads, today best recognizable in the small Piazza dei Crociferi. *Di Trejo*, that is what the Romans started to call the square and the fountain, "the one from the *trejo*," in which *trejo* is *trivio* (from *tre vie*) in dialect: a crossroad for three roads. It was only a small step from *trejo* to *trevi*. Actually, the Trevi Fountain wasn't originally the immense fountain we now know. In the same spot, there used to be a more modest predecessor, a small fountain with three basins into which fresh water flowed from the Aqua Virgo. The Aqua Virgo was so popular that during the Middle Ages special civil servants guarded the water of the Trevi. The city government tasked them with catching so-called *acquaroli*, water thieves. The *acquaroli* allegedly stole large quantities of water from the fountain, which had been paid for by taxpayer's money, only to resell it door-to-door at a high price.

In the fifteenth century, the fountain with three basins was replaced with a new design containing only a single basin, but all three mouths through which the water flowed remained—even in the new, grandiose 1762 fountain that was built in the same spot to overshadow all its predecessors. Still commissioned by Barberini Pope Urban VIII, Bernini made the first sketches for this new Trevi Fountain. All Bernini's ideas were so expensive that the Pope felt compelled to hike the excise duties on wine. Pasquino, who was working overtime during the pontificate of the Barberini Pope, couldn't hold back and said, "Urban makes us pay/much excise on wine./In exchange his citizens now may/drink water from this fountain."[1]

People kept grumbling, and their complaints increased exponentially when they heard Bernini was planning—after he had already stolen quite a lot of material from the city—to pillage a monument from antiquity to obtain the building materials for his new fountain: the tomb of Cecilia Metella on the Via Appia. The uproar this caused was so great that Bernini's designs were deep-sixed. Both Pope Urban VIII and Bernini died before the construction of the Trevi Fountain had begun in earnest. The contract wasn't written out until the early eighteenth century, this time by Pope Clement XII. Nicola Salvi won the pitch and began construction in 1735. As you can immediately tell when standing on the Piazza di Trevi, Salvi was originally a designer of stage sets and found inspiration in Bernini's sketches. With a sense of drama, he made the sea god Oceanus rise up, on his enormous shell, in the middle of the fountain on the tiny plaza. The sea god on his shell is being pulled by two winged horses, symbols of a rough and a calm sea.

[1] Henk Van Gessel, *Pasquino. Spot en satire in Rome* (Amsterdam, 2006).

In the 1960s, Italian cinema made the Trevi Fountain world-famous overnight. In his *La Dolce Vita*, Federico Fellini had Anita Ekberg and Marcello Mastroianni walk into the fountain, a scene lodged in the collective memory of movie aficionados. Later, director Ettore Scola included a small tribute to this iconic scene in his film *C'eravamo Tanti Amati*. In that movie, a group of youngsters passes the Trevi Fountain exactly at the moment Fellini is recording his scene. Throwing coins dates back to the 1950s, after the release of the American movie *Three Coins in the Fountain*. Since then, very few tourists in Rome skip this ritual: turn your back to the fountain and throw a coin with your right hand over your left shoulder, without looking, to ensure that you will one day return to Rome.

XXXVIII

VIA DELLE CARROZZE

CARRIAGES FROM ALL OVER EUROPE

It must have been a terrible endeavor to travel from Western Europe to Rome in the eighteenth century. A sea voyage had its inconveniences and health risks, but traveling by coach over land was dangerous, too. Yet, by stepping into the Via delle Carrozze, we are entering the heart of the eighteenth-century neighborhood that witnessed the extraordinary rise of international cultural tourism in the Eternal City. A clear sign was the studio of Giovanni Battista Piranesi, at the bottom of the early-eighteenth-century Spanish Steps. Piranesi had barely made a living as an etcher in Rome in the mid-eighteenth century. For the first time, he sold etchings (*vedute*) of the most important monuments of the city and its surroundings in large sizes and with enormous success to foreign artists and intellectual "cultural tourists."

Piranesi was born in Venice, and his father, Angelo Piranesi, had been a stonemason. Young Piranesi dreamed of a career as an architect. In 1740, he first came to Rome, together with the Venetian ambassador, Marco Foscarini. His encounter with Rome, especially with the monuments and ruins from antiquity, would change him and his work forever. The times were favorable: Benedict XIV was on the papal throne, a well-loved man known for his intelligence and love of arts and culture. Of course, Rome had always been able to count on visitors, but they often had a specific (religious, diplomatic, artistic, legal, or scientific) purpose. Now the historic capital of Europe could become a pilgrimage site for the intellectual elite. At that time, well-to-do Europeans often enjoyed a classical education. When prosperity and infrastructure permitted it, this education (and upbringing) culminated in a study trip to the origin of classical culture—thus the Grand Tour was born. A visit to the ruins of Rome was one of the highlights of such a trip, a must in the edification of rich young men.

Well-off travelers came to Rome from every corner of Europe, and the demand for the large etchings as souvenirs increased, as did the demand for illustrated travel guides. For Piranesi, it would become an inexhaustible source of income. During his decades-long career, he made etchings of just about all the buildings and ruins in Rome, but the recurrent themes of his *vedute* show that the most popular sights then were not so different from those of today. He often chose the Colosseum, the Forum Romanum, the Trevi Fountain, or the Pantheon as subjects. There's no denying the commercial success of Piranesi's etchings; for better or worse, he did not make history as a great architect but as a talented etcher. When he died, he left behind only a few buildings (the church building and the villa of the Knights of Malta), but more than a thousand etchings.

The Via delle Carrozze was one of the last legs of the endless carriage voyages to Rome, which for many French and British tourists ended on or near the Piazza di Spagna. There were no tourists other than Grand Tourists yet, and most visitors stayed much longer (weeks, even months) in the city than an average city trip lasts nowadays. It comes as no surprise that visitors sought each other out. Soon enough, the eighteenth-century Grand Tourists in Rome gathered in the area around the Spanish Steps. At some point, there were so many British people here that it became known as the *ghetto degli inglesi*. It was not only a meeting place but also a hotbed of creativity for like-minded and well-educated visitors, and a place for exchanging culture and ideas.

Both travelers and carriages needed to recuperate after the long, uncomfortable voyage by coach from Tuscany or other northern Italian regions that were part of the Grand

Tour before their arrival in Rome. The streets leading to the Piazza di Spagna were so narrow that the coaches often suffered much damage. A new form of tourist industry slowly took shape: near the Spanish Steps, several carriage repair shops opened up. If visitors wanted their carriages to be fixed quickly, they were sent to one street in particular. Its name, Via delle Carrozze, the "street of the carriages," still reminds us of the days when damaged coaches came and went through this street.

XXXIX

PIAZZA DI SPAGNA

THE REGULARS OF CAFFÈ GRECO

In 1760, the Greek Nicola della Maddalena opened his Caffè Greco on the Via dei Condotti. One of the rooms of the café, the Omnibus, gives Rome's Grand Tourism a face, or rather, many well-known faces, because none other than Casanova, Goethe, Wagner, Schopenhauer, Stendhal, Lord Byron, and P. B. Shelley were regulars here. In other words, Caffè Greco was a meeting place for the most evocative names in European culture, literature, and art, a world under the influence of Romanticism and undoubtedly a hotbed of ideas.

The street where this famous café is still located, the Via dei Condotti, was relatively new at the time, and its existence is due to the installation of water mains (*condutturi*) below its predecessor, the Via Trinitatis. From then on, these would bring the water from the Aqua Virgo to the Field of Mars, too. The name that disappeared, Via Trinitatis, was much more logical, dating back to the pontificates of Paul III (Alessandro Farnese) and Julius III. It was the new, straight route to the Trinità dei Monti (or, Santissima Trinità al Monte Pincio) church constructed by these two popes. The old street was also much longer than its successor since it comprised the current Via della Fontanella di Borghese and Via del Clementino.

Caffè Greco was one of the last popular addresses on the Via dei Condotti before travelers reached the Piazza di Spagna. The Fontana della Barcaccia (the "fountain of the shipwreck"), which graces the center of the square, was built for Barberini Pope Urban VIII in 1629. The painter and sculptor Pietro Bernini, the father of Gian Lorenzo, was commissioned for the work, and with his son, he designed a fountain that made clever use of the low water pressure by having the water seep from the wreckage. At that time, the square did not have the steps leading to the church or the obelisk in front of it. Those stately, broad stairs were only built between 1723 and 1726, commissioned by Pope Innocent XIII. The idea of bridging the large differences in height by means of steps was first mentioned in the second half of the sixteenth century. Pope Gregory XIII wanted to have stairs "equal to the ones of the *Aracoeli*" (the steps leading to the Santa Maria in Aracoeli church on the Capitoline Hill).

The final design came from Francesco De Sanctis, who was inspired by sketches of one of Bernini's projects that never materialized. The church and the steps are symbolically connected. Just as the Trinità dei Monti is dedicated to the Holy Trinity (*trinità*) (the Father, the Son, and the Holy Spirit), the monumental steps have been divided into three. Immediately following their completion in 1728, part of the Spanish Steps collapsed. The damaged part was quickly fixed, but the architect, De Sanctis, received no more work orders in Rome.

The official Italian name for the Spanish Steps is Scalinata di Trinità dei Monti. So the immense stairs (*scalinata* in Italian) got their name from the church found at the top. Although the steps are called "Spanish," the four-hundred-plus-year-old stones of the church have a French past. French King Louis XII founded the Santissima Trinità in the early sixteenth century, and the abbey and church officially still belong to the French state. The steps and square (Piazza di Spagna) are called "Spanish" because of a seventeenth-century building at Piazza di Spagna 57, where the Spanish embassy at the Holy See is located. The British also left their mark on the Piazza di Spagna: the Keats-Shelley Memorial House was established in the building where John Keats died at age twenty-five after his doctors had sent him to Rome as a cure for his tuberculosis.

Keats was buried, as was his friend Percy Bysshe Shelley, in the only place where Protestants could be buried in Rome: the Cimitero Acattolico. The Church opened up this piece of land on the edge of the city, in the shadow of the Pyramid of Cestius, especially for non-Catholics to be buried. The Campo Cestio, as the Cimitero Acattolico is called today, has become a modest pilgrimage site for fans and admirers of Keats and Shelley, the two most famous and admired poets of British Romanticism, the movement that, following the rational Enlightenment and excessive Baroque periods, (re)claimed a prominent place for originality and the power and beauty of nature. It was the time of Goethe, Beethoven, and Schubert, and of Keats and Shelley. As poets, both were almost the embodiment of the Romantic wind that was blowing through cultural Europe toward the end of the eighteenth century.

XL

PIAZZA DELLA CANCELLERIA

NAPOLEON, THE NEW NERO

Very early in the nineteenth century, the talking statue Pasquino "spoke" in mysterious code, not from his own pedestal, but from a wall nearby. He wrote "NNN" on the Palazzo Doria, where French general Miollis resided at that time. The irritated Frenchman promised a reward to the person who would tell him what those three letters meant. The following day an explanation was added to the wall: NAPOLEONE NUOVO NERONE (Napoleon, the New Nero). The word GRATIS was added. Pasquino did not need a reward.

European politics did not leave Rome unscathed toward the end of the eighteenth century. The year 1789 was the year of the French Revolution, and in Rome, Pius VI (Giovanni Angelo Braschi) was Pope. In 1796, young French general Napoleon invaded Italy. In Rome, he outwitted Pius VI and forced him to sign a humiliating truce. The debt Napoleon imposed on the Vatican amounted to tens of millions of *scudi*, the currency of the Papal States. To pay off this exorbitant amount of money—an average professor made about twenty-five *scudi* a month—Pius VI even pillaged silver from the Gesù, the Jesuit church in Rome. A satirical dialogue between the talking statues Marforio and Pasquino ensued when the French troops looted hundreds of Vatican works of art to take to France: "*È vero che i francesi sono tutti ladri?*"—"*Tutti no, ma buona parte.*"[1] ("Is it true that all Frenchmen are thieves?"—"Not all, but a majority, yes.")

[1] Van Gessel, *Pasquino.*

The pun in Italian, *buona parte* = (Napoleon) Bonaparte, gets lost in translation.

Napoleon was a foreign conqueror on Roman soil, and Pasquino let everybody know that he would not tolerate the French occupier. But in the meantime, the spirit of the French Revolution had taken over the streets of Rome. With the support of the French, the Roman people rose up against the absolute authority of the Pope. A few months later, the French took possession of Rome in its entirety, and they proclaimed it a Roman Republic. As a symbolic action, the new tribunal of this republic was established in the Palazzo della Cancelleria, on the square with the same name, near the Campo de' Fiori. Since the sixteenth century, the Apostolic Chancery had been located in this Renaissance palace (built between 1486 and 1513), but Rome had now been freed from this papal yoke. Pius VI, an octogenarian by then, was expelled from his own Vatican. It turned out that he could not handle traveling anymore. Pius VI died soon thereafter, as an ordinary "citizen," on his way to France.

A new Pope was announced, the seventh Pius—for the first time not in Rome, but in Venice. Most cardinals had fled to Venice, so it only seemed logical to hold the conclave of 1800 there. Pasquino taunted Pius VII because he had opted for a diplomatic solution when he collaborated on a treaty (the Concordat) between the French Church and Rome. He even attended Napoleon's coronation as emperor in 1804. But Pius VII's lenient attitude could not prevent him from coming into conflict with Napoleon again. In 1809, Emperor Napoleon reduced the role of the Papal State to basically one of a French satellite state. The Palazzo della Cancelleria became property of the Imperial Court, and the Pope was expelled from Rome. Subsequently, in less than five years all of Europe had turned against Napoleon, and now it was the emperor himself who was exiled, to Elba. Pius VII returned to the Vatican and highlighted the restored honor of the Papal State by having a new yellow-and-white flag designed. He also hung up marble street signs in all Roman streets. The Palazzo della Cancelleria was returned to the Holy See. It would remain this way until today, apart from a brief period of resurgence of the Roman Republic in 1849. Napoleon was definitively defeated at Waterloo in 1815.

All over Europe, there was no going back: revolutionary movements sprang up everywhere. The Year of the Revolutions, 1848, did not go unnoticed in Rome. The Pope—by now the ninth Pius occupied the Holy See in Vatican City—had even shown himself to be quite the liberal in his policies. But the mostly radical parliament did not accept anything less than a definitive separation of the powers of Church and State. On the steps of the Palazzo della Cancelleria, these radicals stabbed Pellegrino Rossi, prime minister of the Papal State and the foremost advocate of Pius IX. For the second time in half a century, Rome was declared a republic, but, again, it would not survive for very long. In 1849, Napoleon III came to the rescue of the displaced Pope, and Rome came under the authority of the Papal State once more. Pius IX occupied the Pontificate for thirty-one years, longer than any pope before him. Fate and the course of history determined, however, that he would also enter the history books as the last sovereign pope of the Papal State.

XLI

PIAZZALE GARIBALDI

THE BIRTH OF ITALY

Many street names in the old center are unique to the city of Rome, in that they generally do not exist elsewhere in Italy. Those names of Roman streets and squares that are interchangeable with those in other Italian cities are a reflection of the course of history. They refer to a new chapter in the history of the entire nation—the Italian unification, the so-called Risorgimento—as well as to the period preceding it. Starting in that era, men could rise to be heroes of a united Italy instead of only being celebrated in their own city-state or kingdom (Florence, Venice, Naples, Rome). In light of this, it is clear why there is a *via* or *piazza* named after Garibaldi in just about every Italian city.

Liberty, equality, fraternity. Influenced by the political ideals of the French Revolution, a collective striving for national independence took hold in different parts of Europe. Italy had never actually been "Italy." In the boot, there had always been numerous small states, republics, and kingdoms, sometimes governed by foreign rulers. In the mid-nineteenth century, many intellectuals openly regretted the Italian divisions, and even Pope Pius IX held ideas that were almost liberal. For example, he allowed for a certain degree of freedom of the press. He struck a chord with many Italians who started to feel a common unity, and even in a divided Italy, a solidarity movement started slowly to take shape. Pius' weak liberalism could not remove the social and political tensions; later in his career, Pius would gradually shift his position. Soon it became clear how far the radicals were willing to go for their ideals.

Giuseppe Garibaldi valiantly led the nationalists, mostly from the Gianicolo Hill, where you will find today's Piazzale Garibaldi. Who was this combative and fearless Garibaldi, and where was he from? Ironically, Italy's most famous unity fighter was not of Italian origin: he was born in Nice. It was not until his hometown was added to the Kingdom of Sardinia in 1814 that he became Italian in a certain sense—first and foremost, though, he became Sardinian. He was not interested in a career as a physician or a priest, which his parents had wanted him to pursue. Garibaldi desired adventure instead of studies, ideals instead of dogmas. At a young age, he traveled around the world working on merchant ships, and he quickly felt drawn to the nationalist movement of Giuseppe Mazzini.

An early revolution attempt resulted in Garibaldi being sentenced to death, so in 1835 he fled to South America. There he joined the army. In Brazil he met eighteen-year-old Anita. Her full name was Ana Maria, and she was already married. The stories told over time about the meeting between Anita and Garibaldi have taken on somewhat mythical proportions, but the two must have been madly in love with each other. Before long, Anita chose Garibaldi over her husband. On the eve of the Year of the Revolutions, 1848, there were two things of which Garibaldi was convinced: that he was going to board the first ship back to Italy, and that Anita would board with him.

After 1848, when the prime minister of the Papal State, Pellegrino Rossi, was murdered in broad daylight, and Pope Pius IX had to flee, Garibaldi decided to join the revolutionary movement in Rome. For the second time, a *Napoleone* marched on Rome, when Napoleon III helped the Pope find a safe way back to the Vatican. A cannonball in the wall of the San Pietro in Montorio, on the Gianicolo Hill, is a reminder of the bloody battle between Garibaldi and the French in 1849. The French troops defeated the radical revolutionaries, and Garibaldi's troops had to find a safe haven in the mountains outside the city. Despite the objections of the Papal State, the movement for Italian unity grew steadily. The slogan "*Viva Verdi!*" was slowly but surely heard throughout the entire boot. It was the favorite code of the revolutionary nationalists, short for ***Viva Vittorio Emanuele, Re D'Italia***—"Long live Victor Emanuel, King of Italy!"

The fighters for unity saw their perseverance rewarded in 1861: Pius IX, and in his name the Papal State, tacitly accepted the new situation when the United Kingdom of Italy was proclaimed, with Victor Emanuel II as its king and Florence as its capital. Just to be sure, Pius continued to rely on protection by the French troops.

In view of the political situation in Europe, that was not a smart move. In 1870, the Franco-German War broke out. The troops that were to protect the Church and the Pope were needed elsewhere. This was the chance for which the nationalists had been waiting. On September 20, 1870, Victor Emanuel II's troops were at the gates of Rome. They succeeded in smashing a hole in the wall near the Porta Pia. Pius IX knew that his fate was sealed, and that the day he had feared for decades had come. When he heard an enormous bang, he reportedly mumbled "*Consummatum est*" ("it has been completed"), quoting Jesus on the cross. The white flag was waving over Vatican City. Soon thereafter, Romans voted en masse for the city to join the new, unified Italy. After centuries of Vatican dominance, this was the end of papal authority and the Papal State. Pasquino, too, would be silent from then on—he had lost his most important opponent.

The Italian nationalists led by Victor Emanuel II made the Pope a "prisoner of the Vatican." It would take more than fifty years for the Pope and the Church to get back in the good graces of the Italian state, and the sovereignty of Vatican City to be recognized. In 1870, Rome became the new capital of unified Italy, and the new rulers almost immediately hired architects and engineers for a thorough overhaul of the city. This is when the top of Gianicolo Hill was transformed from a battlefield into a park for the public, which it still is today. On the current Piazzale Garibaldi we find, in addition to a splendid view of Rome, an equestrian statue of Garibaldi. The pedestal contains the Italian text ROMA O MORTE—"Rome or death," one of Garibaldi's favorite battle cries. In 1932, Brazil presented to the city of Rome an equestrian statue of Anita (sitting sidesaddle). It was also placed on Gianicolo Hill—as befits a good wife, in the shadow of her husband.

One of the most striking and far-reaching building projects of the architects of the new capital Rome was the monument for Victor Emanuel II, the first king of Italy. After his death, in 1878, a plan was developed, headed up by his successor, Umberto I, to erect a commemorative monument for the "Father of the Nation" that would also honor the spirit of the Risorgimento, through allegorical and symbolic detailing. In 1880, a design competition for the project was announced, but it was not until 1911 that the Vittoriano or Altare della Patria, the name in Italian of the enormous white monument on the current Piazza Venezia, was completed and dedicated by Victor Emanuel III. It is still by far the most salient construction in Rome, and over the years it has acquired some unflattering nicknames: the typewriter, the (false) teeth, the wedding cake. The official inauguration of the Vittoriano coincided with the fiftieth anniversary of Italian unity, and to celebrate its completion, a festive dinner for a small group was organized in the bronze bowels of the equestrian statue of Victor Emanuel II. On November 4, 1921, the Unknown Soldier, a military man who died during the First World War, was laid to rest underneath the statue of Dea Roma (the goddess Rome).

XLII

PIAZZA COLONNA

THE ROMAN BELLE ÉPOQUE

In 1870, Rome became the capital of a united Italy fairly suddenly. Still, calling it a cultural metropolis would be a stretch: popes and citizenry had continuously been fighting each other, and as long as the Pope had the authority, the city was relatively isolated. In September 1870, grand plans were swiftly developed for the future of Rome, with many urban renovations that mainly focused on health, safety, and comfort.

The improving circumstances led to a doubling of the number of inhabitants in a relatively short period of time. A new, self-aware citizenry inhabited the city, which could now grow to become a social and cultural center like in some other European capitals, where the main characters from every episode of Roman history had seemingly acquired a place: from clerics to aristocrats, from intellectuals and scientists to artists, and from journalists to civil servants. Rome experienced its own version of the French Belle Époque, a relatively carefree era on which people would look back with nostalgia after the First World War.

Just as the eighteenth-century Grand Tourists had met in and around Caffè Greco near the Piazza di Spagna, most late nineteenth-century and early twentieth-century travelers liked to gather in the cafés around the Piazza Colonna—named after the ancient column (*colonna*) of Marcus Aurelius in its center. The first experiments with electric streetlights were conducted exactly on this square in 1866. Simultaneously, the idea of "strolling" in the evening entered the Roman street scene, after Baudelaire created the nineteenth-century "stroller" as a literary figure. We can imagine that precisely on this square the paths of, for example, Gabriele D'Annunzio, the most engaged and politically influential writer/poet in Italian history, and the Dutch author Louis Couperus from The Hague, crossed—two outspoken dandies who embodied the intellectual climate of their time. Couperus lived in Rome and Florence for awhile, and he said that he felt as if he had been a "reincarnated Roman from the Imperial Period."

Between February and May 1894, the leading Dutch literary magazine *De Gids* published nearly all of Couperus' travel impressions, including his experiences in Rome. For example, looking out over the city from the Pincian Hill, he described a still-recognizable image of a blanket of domes that is Rome: "Near the bottom of the *viales* and terraces of the Pincio, the great city shapes itself in domes. First, wide, and straight below, the Piazza del Popolo . . . To the left, on the Piazza del Popolo, are the domes of both its churches—Santa Maria to the right—and behind those domes, farther and farther away, yielding to the distance, lie domes, always domes, the round ones, the oval ones, and the flatter ones, a sea of dome-shaped churches."

Winds of change were blowing through D'Annunzio and Couperus' Europe. In Paris, the Eiffel Tower had recently become a proud symbol of progress, and the steam engine was entering its Golden Age. Following Berlin's example, Rome welcomed its first electric tramways. The concept of the "department store" spread from Paris and the United States, and in 1886, La Rinascente opened its doors, diagonally across from the Piazza Colonna. The new, self-aware bourgeoisie (both men and women) followed the latest developments in fashion. After 1914, Rome saw an abrupt end to the world of shop windows, strollers, and innocence, just as the rest of Europe did. During the First World War, Couperus resided in Florence, while D'Annunzio stayed in Rome, where he made the transformation from a literary dandy into a war hero.

Although he spoke of Mussolini disapprovingly, accusing him of plagiarism, D'Annunzio's fanatical nationalism and incendiary speeches made him an important, albeit unintended, source of inspiration for Benito Mussolini, a man whose star had only just begun to rise in Italy.

XLIII

VIA DEI FORI IMPERIALI

MUSSOLINI'S NEW PATH

We have slowly entered twentieth-century Rome. The First World War left deep wounds all over Europe. After 1918, it was understandable that people preferred looking forward rather than backward. The spirit of progress quickly permeated Rome again, visualized by the numerous city renovations. The Corso Vittorio Emanuele II, built in 1886, was connected via the new Foro Argentina to the Via Arenula, opened six years earlier. The person in charge of the archaeological remains that came to light during that work was Benito Mussolini. His interests in this were political rather than personal. Over the course of the 1920s and '30s, it would become apparent that ancient Rome would get an important place in Mussolini's grand plans for the capital of the young nation-state Italy.

Mussolini's new path was literally paved along the imperial forums of Trajan, Augustus, Julius Caesar, and Nerva. In the form of numerous columns, rubble, and remains of temples, these great names from the (early) Roman Imperial Period mark the wide main thoroughfare that connects the Piazza Venezia with the Piazza del Colosseo—the Vittoriano with the Colosseum: the Via dei Fori Imperiali. The street itself is not ancient but has a fascist heritage; Mussolini had it built, seeing himself in the footsteps of those great Roman emperors.

The March on Rome in October 1922, when fascist Blackshirts marched into the city, marked the beginning of a new era in Rome. The fascist movement, headed by Il Duce Mussolini, was taking charge. The party leader had grand plans for Italy, and for Rome in particular. He had always been a gifted speaker and a skilled propagandist. On April 21, 1924, Mussolini gave a public address in the Palazzo dei Conservatori about "Rome's problems" and about the need to restore the "grandeur" of ancient Rome through the *liberazione* ("liberation") of the monuments from antiquity. In other words, Rome's ruins ought to be stripped of later additions as much as possible. Mussolini's message was clear: for the first time since the Golden Age of Emperor Augustus, Italy had again become as great as it was during the Roman Empire.

Mussolini's fascist ideology and theories were manifested in the Roman cityscape. The construction plans and projects for the city brought new infrastructural advantages, but they also carried a considerable ideological weight, and their main purpose was directly to link ancient Rome to the fascist present. Nothing is as modern as the past: Mussolini cherry-picked events from history, and in his propaganda he cleverly joined together elements that fit his narrative and supported his message. The past was brutally taken out of context, and in a new framework it was given a twentieth-century life and meaning. Historians have extensively studied the way Mussolini dealt with ancient Rome, precisely because it is so telling for the general ideology of Il Duce and for the social, political, and societal developments in fascist Italy.

Mussolini dreamed of a new Italian Empire, and as is often the case with ambitious leaders, his dreams were grandiose. Rome was to become a symbol of his imperial ambitions and of his philosophy, which he wanted to roll out, in part, by building two new roads. The Via del Mare was one of them: a new road that led from the Piazza Venezia straight to the old Roman port city of Ostia. In 1932, construction was begun on the second one: the Via dell'Impero, the Road of the Empire. The *impero* referred to here was the Italian Empire. Mussolini had started to use the Palazzo Venezia as his working palace, on the square by the same name, at the bottom of the Vittoriano. The construction of the broad road that connected the Piazza Venezia and the Colosseum allowed him a distant view of the latter, that grand monument of ancient Rome. As a child of his time, Mussolini loved military parades. The new boulevard proved especially well suited for that purpose.

It would be difficult to imagine the amount of destruction and demolition required for the construction of the Via dell'Impero if not for surviving photographs and moving pictures that document the period. During the demolition, archaeologists reportedly visited Mussolini on a nearly daily basis to request research access, but Mussolini was not interested in the intrinsic value that could be ascribed to the Roman remains. This became clear when Mussolini kicked out the archaeologists: the Via dell'Impero project was time-sensitive, and the construction pits were partially closed before any archaeologist could inspect them. Most Romans didn't lose any sleep over it. Following the example of Pope Julius II's Via Giulia, the new Via dell'Impero would be "the most beautiful street in the world," and, literally, a showpiece for the city. A stroll along the new street—from the Tomb of the Unknown Soldier to the majestic ruins of the Colosseum—would be loaded with symbolic meaning. The Via dell'Impero itself, symbol of the new order of the fascist regime in Rome, was the axis that inextricably connected all those elements from Rome's past to each other and to Mussolini's Rome.

When Adolf Hitler paid Rome a visit in 1938, Mussolini was glad he had sped up the construction of his boulevard. Hitler was treated to impressive military parades, which must have increased Il Duce's prestige in the eyes of the Führer. At times, Mussolini's fascism was perhaps a source of inspiration for the Nazis, but in the end, Italians were also in principle inferior in Hitler's eyes, higher ranked than slaves, gypsies, or Jews, but still subordinate to the superior race. So, there was a need to impress Hitler. Mussolini's dream parade was much grander than reality could manage. He was faced with a shortage of soldiers, and he secretly had the same troops march more than once along the Via dell'Impero. They marched in a circle past the Colosseum, where they would quickly put on a different uniform. Some of the arms they were carrying were made of cardboard, and where the Via dell'Impero had not been completed Mussolini placed some sort of stage scenery, to avoid showing any dilapidated houses.

Hitler's visit also inspired Mussolini to place five enormous stone maps against the exterior wall of the Basilica of Maxentius and Constantine on the Forum Romanum. These maps, four of which survived, show the development and geographical expansion of the Roman Empire. The fifth map depicted the fascist Italian Empire, the *impero* of Mussolini, to which Ethiopia could be added in 1936. Italy had occupied Eritrea since 1882, and Somalia since 1889. In between lay Haile Selassie's Abyssinia (now Ethiopia), which, after an entirely unequal battle, was stomped on by fascist boots and annexed by Italy.

Mussolini hung the maps along his Via dell'Impero because, reportedly, a marble map of Rome hung here in antiquity, parts of which can still be admired today in the Capitoline Museums. After the Second World War, the city of Rome had the fifth map removed. The name of Mussolini's showcase street was changed to the name it still carries today: the Via dei Fori Imperiali, the Road of the Imperial Forums.

XLIV

VIA DELLA CONCILIAZIONE

RECONCILIATION STREET

The 1911 inauguration of the enormous, snow-white Altare della Patria celebrated the unification of Italy. It also indirectly commemorated another historic event that had a drastic impact on Italy, and especially on Rome: the end of the secular authority of the Pope. The Italian state and the Vatican did not reconcile until 1929, when the Lateran Treaty stated that the fascists recognized the territorial independence and sovereign status of Vatican City. From now on, their regime could count on papal recognition—in spite of the fact that some fascist views were irreconcilable with the ideas of the Catholic Church. It is after this great reconciliation (*conciliazione*) that the road built in 1936, which connected the Ponte Sant'Angelo and St. Peter's Square, was named: the Via della Conciliazione.

The path of the new street was known in antiquity as the Via Cornelia, a road just outside the city walls, along which there were numerous graves. It was not mentioned again until the early twentieth century. When Pope Pius XI (1922–1939) communicated that it was his wish to be buried as close to Saint Peter's tomb as possible when he died, it was decided that the crypt below the main altar of St. Peter's Basilica had to be lowered. The tomb of Saint Peter had to be exactly below Bernini's baldachin. For the first time in the modern era, excavations were going to be done on this historically rich site. Soon, they found remains of graves from the Roman Era, as well as remains from the older basilica and the commemorative monument that had been constructed near the grave.

By 1940, the archaeological dig below St. Peter's and the search for the original grave of Saint Peter had still not been completed. In that year, the Vatican researchers finally made the find for which they had been longing. It was only a small box, which, when opened, revealed a few bones and some frayed pieces of cloth. When examined thoroughly, the contents turned out to be the mortal remains of an elderly man. The frayed cloth stemmed from a purple dress with interwoven gold threads. There is even a (tall) tale floating around the Vatican catacombs that the box contained all the bones of a man except for those of his feet. The logic works like this: if Saint Peter was actually hanging upside down on the cross, the gravediggers would have cut off the feet to remove the body from the cross. Despite academic resistance, Pope Paul VI announced publicly, in 1968, that the grave of Apostle Peter, buried long ago on the Via Cornelia, had been found.

Mussolini certainly did not have Saint Peter's tomb on his mind in 1936. Until then, pilgrims and other travelers to Rome had more or less meandered their way through the different streets of the Borgo, only to find themselves, rather suddenly, face-to-face with St. Peter's Basilica. The construction of the Via della Conciliazione created a symmetrical one-point perspective, so that visitors could approach the square and the basilica from a large distance and with awe. For this project, it seems clear that Mussolini was inspired for the first time by the Nazi architecture of Albert Speer. Construction projects that had been going on for years showed little resemblance to that, and, if anything, new projects had shown a modern streak. Examples are, in the North, the forum of Mussolini (Foro Mussolini), with its Stadio dei Marmi (today's Foro Italico), and, in South Rome, the futuristic, second-city-like area EUR (Esposizione Universale di Roma), with its "squared Colosseum." In the '30s, Hitler's influence on Mussolini's thoughts and actions had increased. Although racial theories had never been part of fascist philosophy, Roman versions of the Nuremberg Laws were introduced two years after the construction of the Via della Conciliazione: Jews were barred from certain professions, and they were stripped of their citizenship. Hitler's invasion of Poland marked the beginning of the Second World War, and Mussolini's declaration of war on the United States marked the beginning of Italy's involvement.

XLV

VIA NICOLA ZABAGLIA

THE LAST TORCHBEARER

There is a small, insignificant story line that runs across the dark side of fascist Roman history. It is a story in the margin of the big events. It is not told very often anymore, knowing how trivial it turned out to be in light of the many deaths caused by the war that was about to break out. It must, nevertheless, have been a dramatic experience for bystanders when, in 1938, someone fell off the dome of St. Peter's.

The actual main characters of the small history of this incident are the dark-grey, tapered basalt cobblestones covering the streets and squares of Rome. They even have a name: *sampietrini*. Tourists are often especially warned about the stones: when it rains, they can be treacherously slippery. Some guides of Rome tell us furthermore that the name *sampietrini* stems from the fact that they were first used to pave St. Peter's Square. This reportedly happened in 1725, after Pope Benedict XIII almost fell out of his carriage—the boulders were uneven, and the square was covered with dangerous holes. The Pope ordered Siena-born Lodovico Segardi to repave the square and to use the local volcanic stone type that has come to characterize Rome in its entirety.

The origin of the word *sampietrini* dates back further than that. It is a reference to the Confraternita dei Sampietrini, a society of masons and construction workers employed by the Fabbrica di San Pietro, the building and maintenance company of St. Peter's Basilica that has forever been the employer of all laborers, artists, and restorers involved in St. Peter's. For example, Lodovico Segardi, who had to repave St. Peter's Square, was an overseer at the Fabbrica di San Pietro between 1713 and 1726. The Fabbrica still exists, and until barely one hundred years ago, the Sampietrini were tasked with lighting all the torches on St. Peter's Square on religious holidays and during other special celebrations. In 1938, the year of Hitler's visit to Rome, one of the members of the Confraternita dei Sampietrini slipped when he had to light the torches around the dome of St. Peter's Basilica. He fell and smashed into the ground below, prompting Pius XII to have the torches replaced by electric lights.

Only a few *sampietrini* have received the honor of their own street name in Rome. In 1686, Nicola Zabaglia was first employed by the Fabbrica di San Pietro. Zabaglia (1664–1750) started as a simple mason, but he soon climbed the ranks, due especially to his talent for designing construction machines and scaffolding, obviously very useful tools in building and maintenance. His technical ingenuity and the seemingly endless possibilities that he envisioned as an inventor and engineer yielded strong admiration in early-seventeenth-century Rome. His work was immortalized, for example, in the book *Castelli e ponti di Maestro Nicola Zabaglia*, which was published in 1743.

Zabaglia was so good that he was given an office in the "attic" of St. Peter's Basilica, exactly above its central nave. From there he could monitor the maintenance activities of the employees whose supervisor he had become (stonemasons, masons, and carpenters). Because he had gathered so many employees around him and displayed great practical and organizational insight, Nicola is seen by many as one of the founders of the Confraternita dei Sampietrini. The Fabbrica had been around for at least a century (Michelangelo also worked at and with the Fabbrica di San Pietro), but it was Nicola Zabaglia, who provided a clearly defined role for the Sampietrini and turned them from simple employees into famous and skilled building experts, after whom a street in the Testaccio quarter was named.

XLVI

LARGO 16 OTTOBRE 1943

THE "EVACUATION" OF THE JEWISH GHETTO

It was clear that Mussolini initially did not think much of Hitler's theory of race. There were Jews among the members of the Fascist Party, and Il Duce had publicly declared that the entire concept of "race" was largely a man-made idea and that Jews had been inhabitants of Rome since its earliest history. There are still Romans who consider the current Jewish inhabitants descendants of the "oldest inhabitants of Rome"—more or less the only "true" remaining Romans.

If you are looking for traces of where Jewish history and the city of Rome's past intersect, you may find yourself at Titus' arch on the Forum Romanum, at the beginning of the Via Sacra. The marble honorary arch was built around 81 CE, and it depicts the military victory of Titus and Vespasian in Jerusalem. On that occasion, in 70 CE, the temple of Jerusalem was completely destroyed and ransacked. The conquest of Jerusalem ended a long period of war in Judea. A famous scene on one of the two pillars of the relief-covered arch of Titus shows how Roman soldiers pillaged the temple of Jerusalem—the menorah still clearly visible. Because it had become a symbol of humiliation and of the diaspora, many Jews refused to walk underneath the arch until the founding of the state of Israel in 1948. Today, nobody can walk underneath it anyway.

Some fifteen centuries later, a dark period began for the Jewish community in Rome: Pope Paul IV decreed by bull, on July 14, 1555, that God had condemned the Jews in Rome for their "crimes" to "eternal slavery." In less than three months, he built walls and gates in order to close off the so-called Jewish ghetto. Originally, there were five gates, intended to make it easy for Jewish inhabitants to leave the area during the day, but to lock them in at night. The Portico d'Ottavia, built around 27 BCE, commissioned by Emperor Augustus and named after his sister Octavia Minor, was put back in service as one of the gates. A second gate was located across from the Santa Maria della Pietà, near the Ponte Fabricio, the oldest bridge in Rome still in use. It connects the bank of the Tiber and Tiber Island. The three other gates were situated on the Via della Fiumara and near the Piazza Giudea. Today, little or nothing is left of that wall or those gates, but, in the area they used to encompass, the Jewish community is alive and well. Numerous restaurants feature the best of Judeo-Roman cuisine.

Nowadays, the Via del Portico d'Ottavia is in the heart of the ghetto. Along that street, near its intersection with the Via Catalana, there is a street sign that reads LARGO 16 OTTOBRE 1943. The reason the people commemorate that particular Saturday is due to yet another very dark day in the history of the Jewish community in Rome. On that day, October 16, 1943, early in the morning, the SS raided the Via del Portico d'Ottavia. Herbert Kappler, head of the SS in Rome, had received an order to "evacuate" the ghetto, straight from Berlin, on September 25. Strangely enough, he did not immediately carry out the order. Instead, on the day he received the order, he summoned Ugo Foa, president of the Jewish community, and Dante Almansi, president of the united Jewish communities of Italy, in an attempt to be "bribed." Kappler himself was not present; he sent a noncommissioned officer in his place. Internally, the Germans had already decided not to execute the order right away, but, because the Jewish representatives did not know that, they were willing to offer quite a bit of gold in order to save the community.

Having given their gold, the Jewish community could feel (relatively) safe for a moment. In early October, German

SS officer Theo Dannecker was sent to Rome to carry out the roundup anyway. Dannecker blindly followed the order. The souls of 1,024 people, among whom numbered at least two hundred children, were apprehended in the ghetto on October 16. Whether the Vatican stood by in silence while this dramatic chapter from Roman history was unfolding is hard to say. Later it was discovered that Pope Pius XII had been blackmailed; the Nazis used for leverage the eight hundred or so Jews hiding in churches and convents all over Europe, which in 1943 was for the most part occupied by the Nazis. The ghetto in Rome was left to fend for itself. The 1,024 Jews who had been arrested were taken to Tiburtina Station and put on a train to Auschwitz, where they arrived six days later. Fifteen men and one woman returned from Poland; none of the others survived.

XLVII

VIA RASELLA

TEN ITALIANS FOR EVERY GERMAN

On a brisk January morning in 2012, a small group of people gathered at 2 Via Urbana. A cobblestone, a *sampietrino*, was officially dedicated to the memory of Pietro Pappagallo, the priest who lived here and who offered a home to whoever needed it during the Nazi occupation of Rome. Pappagallo was betrayed by a German spy and executed near the so-called Fosse Ardeatine on March 24, 1944, almost sixty-eight years earlier. The laying of the *sampietrino* inaugurated a project to commemorate all the victims of that infamous mass execution.

As they were elsewhere in Europe on March 23, 1944, the streets of Rome were filled with German soldiers. In the Via Rasella, just northeast of the Trevi Fountain, the atmosphere was tense on that particular day. A bomb exploded while an SS battalion was marching through the Via Rasella. Thirty-two members of the SS Polizei Regiment "Bozen" died in the attack. The number of casualties would climb a bit in the hours after the attack, when several soldiers succumbed to their injuries. The assault was claimed by the GAP (Gruppo di Azione Patriottica) partisans, a resistance group that used violence to fight Nazism and fascism in the streets of Rome.

Kurt Mälzer was the German commander on duty. Shocked and in a heightened state of indignation, he reported the attack. The message reached Hitler, who burst out in anger. The alleged merciless order from Hitler was that within twenty-four hours one hundred Italians were to be executed for every fallen German soldier. Herbert Kappler, head of the intelligence agency, the *Sicherheitsdienst*, reduced the number. The final disciplinary action was ten Italians for every German. A raid was held in the Via Rasella; randomly selected Jews and passersby were added to a list drawn up earlier to get to the number 330, ten times the number of Germans who died due to the bomb attack, either directly or indirectly. Among them was Don Pietro Pappagallo.

A grisly episode marks the end of these events, which all took place within twenty-four hours. The 335 sentenced to death (five had been added by mistake) were transported to the Fosse Ardeatine, a complex of caves just outside the center of Rome. They were bound together in groups of five and led through the caves by the firing squad. On their knees, the men were shot in the neck. Every new group was forced to kneel on top of those shot before them, so that orderly stacks would be formed. As soon as all 335 Italians had been killed, the Germans closed off the cave by exploding a pile of sticks of dynamite near the entrance. The mass execution took place only twenty-three hours after the attack in the Via Rasella, obviously without any form of trial or public announcement. After the war, the Via Adolfo Hitler, which connected the Porta San Paolo and the Stazione Ostiense, which was especially built for Hitler's visit, was renamed the Viale delle Cave Ardeatine.

After the war, in 1948, police chief Herbert Kappler was sentenced to life in prison. In the '70s, he was diagnosed with cancer, for which he was treated in the military hospital on Celio Hill in Rome. On August 15, 1977, an official holiday in Italy, Kappler's wife helped him escape from the hospital. She had smuggled a bag full of tools into his room. Kappler was sick and by then was seventy years old, but he succeeded in rappelling from the twelfth floor of the hospital. Due to his illness, he weighed less than one hundred pounds.

A few days later, Kappler arrived at his wife's house in Germany, where friends gave them a hearty reception. Kappler even granted some interviews. Italy insisted that

Germany extradite Kappler based on the fact that he was a war criminal, but that request was denied. According to the Germans, Kappler had the right to flee.

Six months later, on February 28, 1978, Kappler died. He is buried in the local cemetery, in Lüneburg, where friends and admirers gave his casket the Nazi salute. In 2011, Kappler's son Ekehard gave an interview to an Italian publication, shedding new light on the former police chief's escape.

After the war, a national memorial was set up at the Fosse Ardeatine. On March 24, an annual commemoration takes place here, marking the events that followed the bomb explosion in the Via Rasella. One of the houses along the Via Rasella, near the intersection with the Via del Boccaccio, contains bullet holes as silent witnesses of these events.

XLVIII

VIA VITTORIO VENETO

A STREET AS A MOVIE SET; A MOVIE SET AS A STREET

Few streets in the center of Rome exude a bohemian ambiance like the Via Margutta. Steps away from the bustling crowds, it is amazingly calm here, nearly always overwhelmingly quiet. The studios and workshops that have settled over time in this artists' street give it its vivacity. Near the workshop of *er marmoraro*, the stonemason of the Via Margutta, you find the building that made the street world famous. House number 51 is Joe's house from the movie *Roman Holiday* (*Vacanze Romane*). One of the oldest buildings of the Via Margutta, number 110, was once occupied by the man who, like no other, has put post-World War II Rome on the map: Federico Fellini.

In 1945, communist partisans apprehended Mussolini while he was fleeing to a foreign country. He was shot dead, together with his mistress. Hanging upside down on meat hooks, their bodies were flogged and abused in Milan. The war was over, and Italy had been freed from the German occupier and Mussolini's fascist regime. Europe was preparing once more for a time to nurse its wounds, to heal, and to reconstruct. In spite of the actions by Allied bombers, the recapturing of Rome had miraculously destroyed very little of the city's historic heritage. New cultural and artistic movements sprouted up on fascist soil: movie park Cinecittà, founded by Mussolini in 1937, became a kind of Hollywood on the Tiber in the '50s and '60s. On top of the ruins of the war, a completely contrasting world of movie stars and jet setters was born. The center of this jet set of mid-twentieth-century Italian cinema was the chic and sophisticated Via Vittorio Veneto.

Shooting movies in the Roman film studios of Cinecittà was so appealing that both Italians and Americans (such as Fellini, Coppola, and Scorsese) loved working there. The production costs were relatively low, and then, of course, there was the irresistible draw of the Eternal City as backdrop and place to stay. International productions turned out classics such as *Ben Hur* (1959) and *Cleopatra* (1963), which were shot in Cinecittà (as was the more recent successful BBC series *Rome*). Studio 5 was the heart and paradise of Fellini's fantasy world: "A space to be filled, a world to be created," he said. He shot his most famous movies, such as *La Dolce Vita* (1960), in Studio 5. The setting of the movie was, fittingly, the Via Vittorio Veneto—which Fellini had replicated in its entirety.

La Dolce Vita is considered one of Fellini's most "accessible" movies. With the Via Vittorio Veneto as backdrop, major roles are played by society reporter Marcello Rubini (Marcello Mastroianni) and foreign movie star Sylvia (Anita Ekberg). In the movie, Rubini dreams of a career as a literary author, but for now he is earning a living as a tabloid journalist. Looking for celebrity gossip, he lingers around the Via Veneto, the epicenter of "the good life," where posh Italians meet at the Café de Paris, and sophisticated Americans on the terrace of Doney. It is a bizarre, Fellinian irony that the street where, in real life, the movie's actors enjoyed each other's company after a day of filming in Cinecittà, was the setting for his movie about that new world of movie stars.

Emerging at the same time as phenomena like movie stars and the jet set in the world of Italian international cinema were the photographers who have followed closely behind ever since. We now refer to these photographers with the Italian umbrella name *paparazzi*. The word is derived from a Fellinian character. In *La Dolce Vita*, we watch how Marcello Rubini continually has to work his way through throngs of aggressive photographers; we also meet the boldest among them, Paparazzo. Pushy photographers worldwide are still named after this Fellini character.

The most well-known and iconic scene from *La Dolce Vita* does not feature the Via Vittorio Veneto, the street that was so precisely replicated in Cinecittà's Studio 5. The famous clip in which Anita Ekberg walks into the Trevi Fountain (followed by a spellbound Mastroianni) was the only scene shot in the center of Rome. The *dolce vita* that Fellini recorded is long gone. One needs a healthy dose of imagination to still catch even a glimpse of its worldly past along the Via Vittorio Veneto, let alone at the Trevi Fountain.

XLIX

VIA MICHELANGELO CAETANI

THE YEARS OF LEAD

On December 12, 1969, at 4:55 pm, a bomb went off in the Via Vittorio Veneto. For the first time in its history, Rome was the target of a terrorist attack. Within thirty minutes, two more bombs exploded, near the Altare della Patria. At the same time, the news from Milan was slowly trickling in that shortly past 4:30, two attacks there had taken the lives of seventeen Italians. Thus began the *Anni di Piombo* ("Years of Lead"), which lasted ten years, with five enormous explosions in the two most important cities of Italy.

As Rome became Hollywood on the Tiber after the Second World War, Europe increasingly felt the grip of the Cold War. In the fight against communism led by the United States, Italy was a participant on the political playing field in the '60s and '70s. Its communist party was relatively popular, despite the fact that the Allied Forces had done everything they could to promote the Christian Democrats (the Democrazia Cristiana party, or DC) after liberating Italy. In their efforts to keep the DC in power, the US focused on a "strategy of tension." For example, an investigative commission established (years after the fact) that the CIA aided the fascist terrorist group responsible for the attacks of 1969. The real purpose was to trigger a response from the extreme-left-wing communists.

The response came in the form of an attack claimed by the Red Brigades (Brigate Rosse), which was founded in 1970. During the ensuing *Anni di Piombo*, Italians were literally caught in the middle between the extreme right and the extreme left. The terrorist attacks, killings, and kidnappings that followed December 1969 claimed hundreds of victims. The most well-known victim was the leader of the DC, and ex-prime minister, Aldo Moro. Ironically, he had just sought a rapprochement with the communists. On March 16, 1978, he was kidnapped in broad daylight, on his way to parliament in Rome. Moro's five security guards were all killed during the hostage taking.

Aldo Moro was held hostage for fifty-five days, during which the famous photo of him in front of the flag of the Red Brigade was released. The terrorists had captured the media's attention. Although Moro was one of the most important politicians of his time, many suspected that the State purposely did little to free him from the hands of the terrorists. Not only the communist party but also some DC members were willing to sacrifice Moro. In any case, the government refused to negotiate with the kidnappers, despite urgent written requests from Moro himself.

On May 9, 1978, the Via Michelangelo Caetani became the setting of the horrifying finale of the Moro case. This street was named after a nineteenth-century politician, but it became a headline in world news thanks to the twentieth-century politician who was held hostage. Enter this street, and about halfway in, diagonally across from the entrance of the Palazzo Mattei di Giove, you will see a portrait of Moro in bronze. A plaque tells you why that portrait is hanging here. It marks the spot where they found the red Renault 4 with the bullet-riddled body of Aldo Moro in the back. The symbolism of the place where the body of Moro was left behind—equidistant between the headquarters of the DC (on the Piazza del Gesù) and the communist party (on the Via delle Botteghe Oscure)—was obvious to everyone in Rome in 1978.

Aldo Moro's portrait in the Via Caetani still reminds us of the violent end he met; it marked the beginning of the end of the *Anni di Piombo.* The bloodiest year, 1980, during which more than one hundred deaths were mourned, was the last of the "years of lead." Not long thereafter, the leaders of the Brigate Rosse were put behind bars. Over the years, and thanks to testimony from imprisoned informers (*pentiti*), not only of extreme right-wing groups, but also *brigatisti* and members of gangs such as the Magliana, more and more details have come to light about the Moro case. Some stones, however, still remain unturned.

L

PIAZZA AUGUSTO IMPERATORE (II)

A GAS STATION IN THE HEART OF ROME

Fellini's imagination, and his successful movies in the '50s and '60s such as *Roman Holiday*, brought Rome back onto Europe's radar. When the Berlin Wall fell in the late '80s and the Iron Curtain was dropped, the "strategy of tension" of the *anni di piombo* became a thing of the past. Mass tourism was gaining momentum: icons of the city, like the Colosseum, St. Peter's Basilica, and the Trevi Fountain, started increasingly to exert their appeal on travelers of all varieties. The city modernized, but since Mussolini, not a single construction project had been started in the old center of Rome. Not until the turn of the century did that change. In line with the new zeitgeist, this innovation came from America.

Just like other cities, Rome was faced with modern problems. In the mid-1990s, it was found that car exhaust and increasing temperatures had seriously threatened the Ara Pacis, the centuries-old Peace Altar of Augustus. In 1995, the city of Rome decided that it was high time (and a necessity) to replace its encasing. Since 1938, this had consisted of a cover and wall around it, designed by the architect Ballio Morpurgo. Between June and September of that year, he gathered the puzzle pieces of the ruins of the Ara Pacis and put them on a platform, surrounded by a portico. While doing so, he had the complete text of the *Res Gestae*, the Emperor Augustus' public testament, affixed to one of the walls. For the symbolism to come full circle, the (re)inauguration of the monument was held on September 23, Augustus' birthday. The revival of the Ara Pacis was part of the Piazza Augusto Imperatore "liberation project," for which Mussolini had wiped an entire Roman neighborhood off the map. The square was created around the overgrown mausoleum of Augustus. The galleries constructed on three sides around the square are typical examples of strict fascist architecture. On one of the facades, you can still find an inscription glorifying Mussolini's construction project, flanked by two "Victoria figures" carrying *fasces*, the bundles of rods that were fascist symbols.

Despite Mussolini's efforts, the health of the monuments of Augustus' Rome seriously deteriorated after the fascist era. The Piazza Augusto Imperatore became rundown, a place to be avoided after dark. Had Augustus been able to turn over in his grave (his remains had not been there for a long time), his view would mainly have consisted of hobos, prostitutes, and drug addicts—not a very imperial view. The new construction project that started in the '90s was born out of necessity. Yet, it inevitably became another fraught and symbolic chapter in the fascinating history of the Piazza Augusto Imperatore.

The commission for the design of the new housing for the Ara Pacis went to Richard Meier, a famous American architect, who also designed The Hague's city hall. The mayor of Rome at the time, Rutelli, in charge of the project, must have known that choosing a non-Italian architect with a preference for modern, sleek, transparent constructions would cause an uproar. For at least half a century, not one modern structure had been built in the historic center of Rome, and now the symbol of the *pax romana* was going to be handled by a representative of the *pax americana*. Nevertheless, the plan was adopted, and Walter Veltroni, Rutelli's successor, had the honor of officially opening the renovated museum on April 21, 2005 (Rome's 2,758th birthday). Many Romans thought the building was very ugly. Intellectuals such as Giorgio Muratore (professor in the history of architecture) and Antonio Tamburino (an urban planning instructor) called the entire project "the worst possible intervention." As always, politics played a role, too: the initiative for "project Meier" came from the very left-wing city government of Rome, so for right-wing parties it was a nonstarter. Silvio Berlusconi called the museum *una mostruosità*, "a monstrosity."

The construction of the new Ara Pacis museum was interrupted four times. A highly ranked official went on a hunger strike in an effort to stop the entire project, and in October 2005, several architects sent an open letter to the Italian newspaper *Corriere della Sera*, in which they warned against the "invasion of foreign architects." The controversy has died down by now, but opponents still disparagingly refer to "the gas station" when they are talking about the museum of the Ara Pacis on the Piazza Augusto Imperatore.

THE HISTORY OF ROME IN FIVE WALKS

The streets in this book follow the history—not the most logical walking route. If you want to stay with the spirit of the book while walking through Rome, you can follow (one of) these historic routes. They will lead you past a large part of these fifty streets.

Walk 1

IN THE FOOTSTEPS OF CLASSICAL ROME

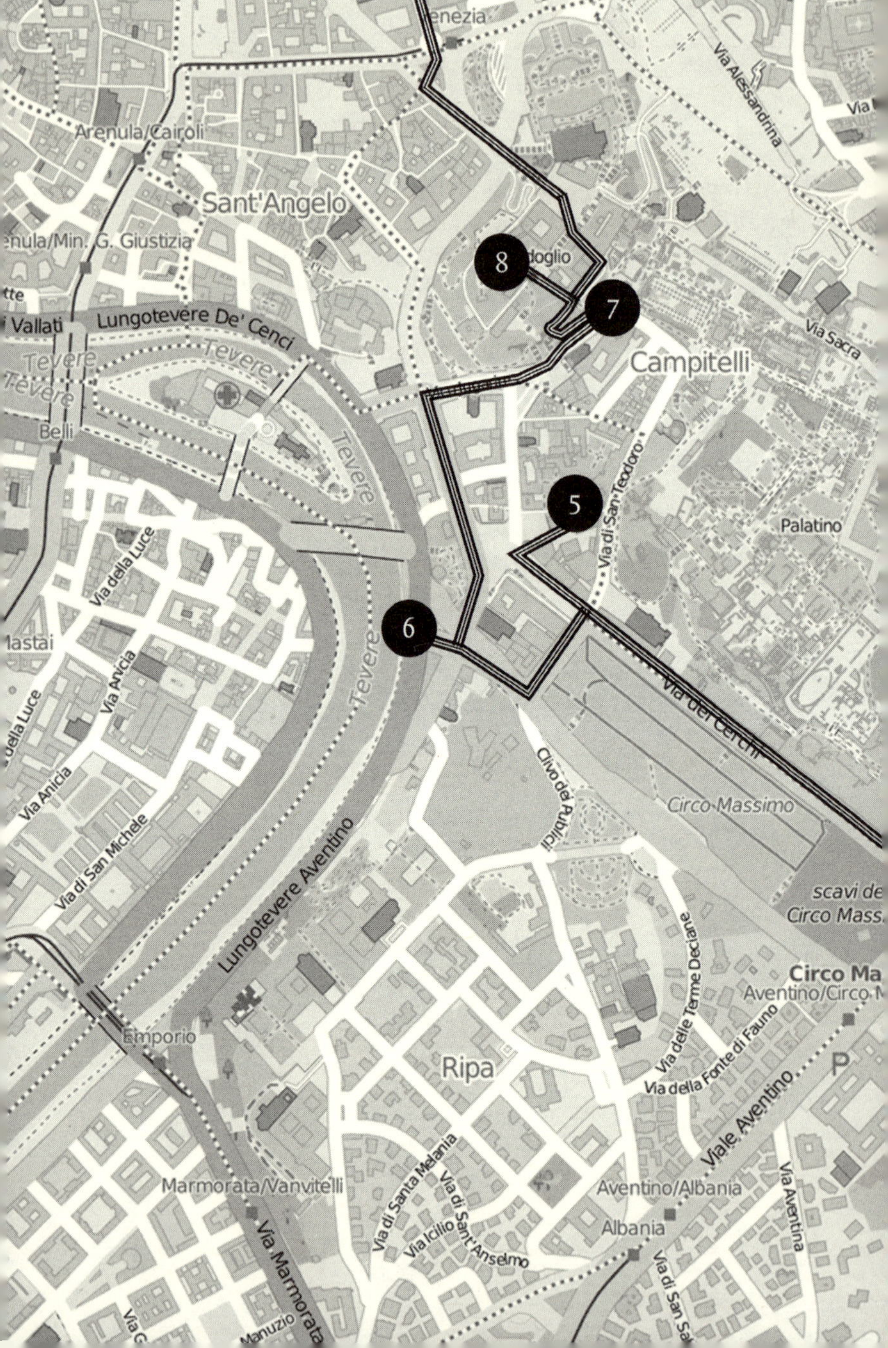

1. Piazza della Suburra / X
2. Viale della Domus Aurea / XVI
3. Via Sacra / XVIII
4. V. delle Terme di Caracalla / XIX
5. Via del Velabro / III
6. De Tiber / I
7. Via Monte Tarpeo / II
8. Via del Tempio di Giove / IV
9. Via del Piè di Marmo / XII

Some sights along the way:
Colosseum
Forum Romanum
Thermae of Caracalla
Capitoline Hill
Capitoline Museums
Tiber Island

Also near this route:
Via Mecenate (XIV)
Via della VII Coorte (XV)
Piazza dei Cavalieri di Malta (XXIII)
Piazza del Campidoglio (XXVIII)

Walk 2

IN THE FOOTSTEPS OF THE POPES AND THE RENAISSANCE

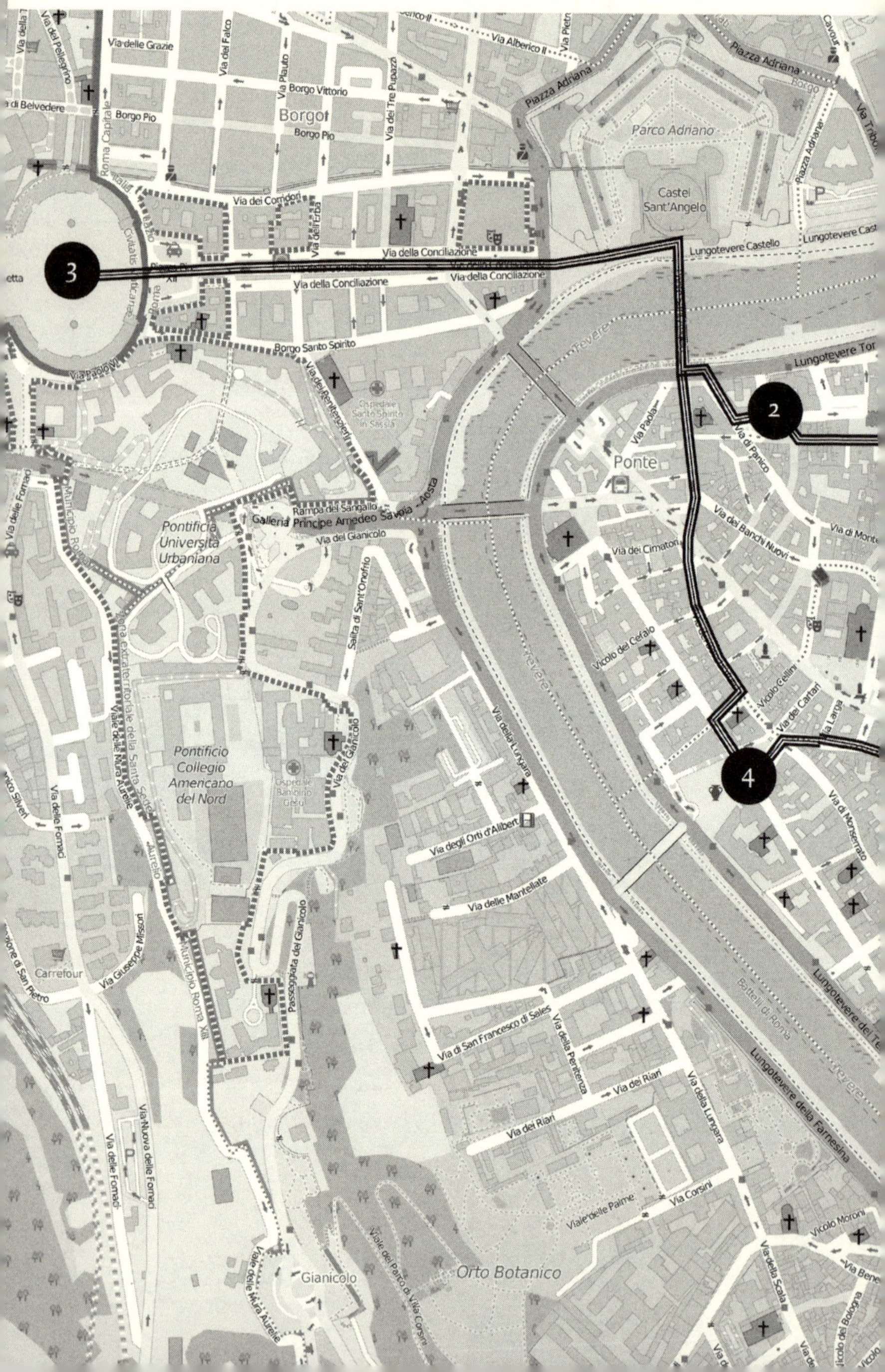

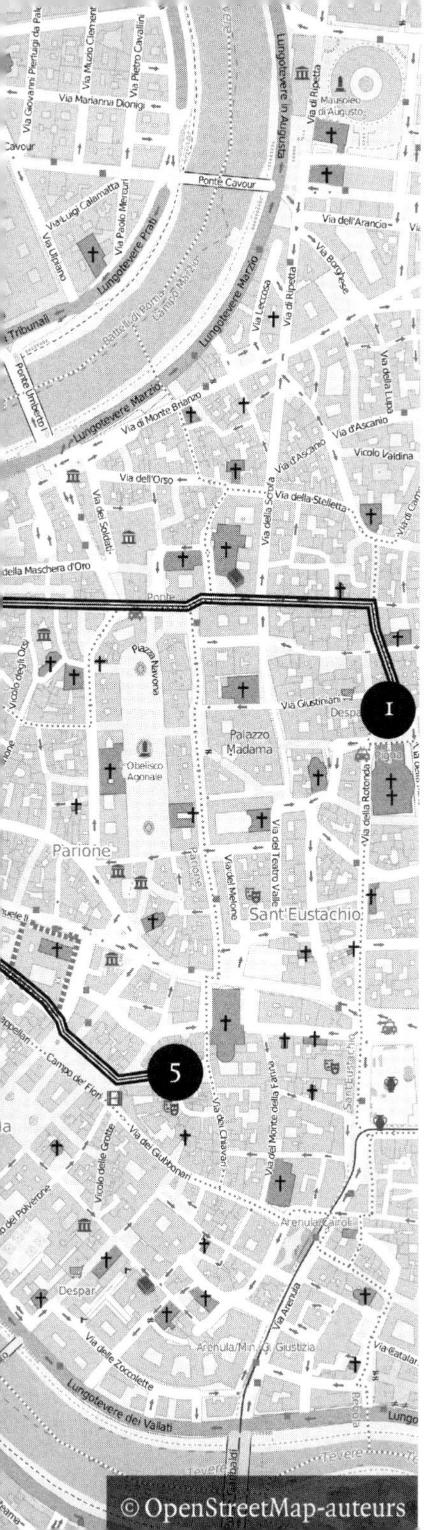

1 Piazza della Rotonda / XXXI

2 Via dei Coronari / XXVI

3 Piazza San Pietro / XXXIV

4 Via Giulia / XXVII

5 Campo de' Fiori / XXIX

Some sights along the way:
Pantheon
Castel Sant'Angelo
The Vatican
Vatican Museums
Campo de' Fiori

Also near this route:
Via del Corso (XXV)
Piazza del Teatro di Pompeo (IX)
Via Cola di Rienzo (XXIV)
Piazza Navona (XXXIII)
Via della Conciliazione (XLIV)
Passetto di Borgo (XXII)
Piazza dei Protomartiri (XVII)

Walk 3

IN THE FOOTSTEPS OF BERNINI AND THE BAROQUE

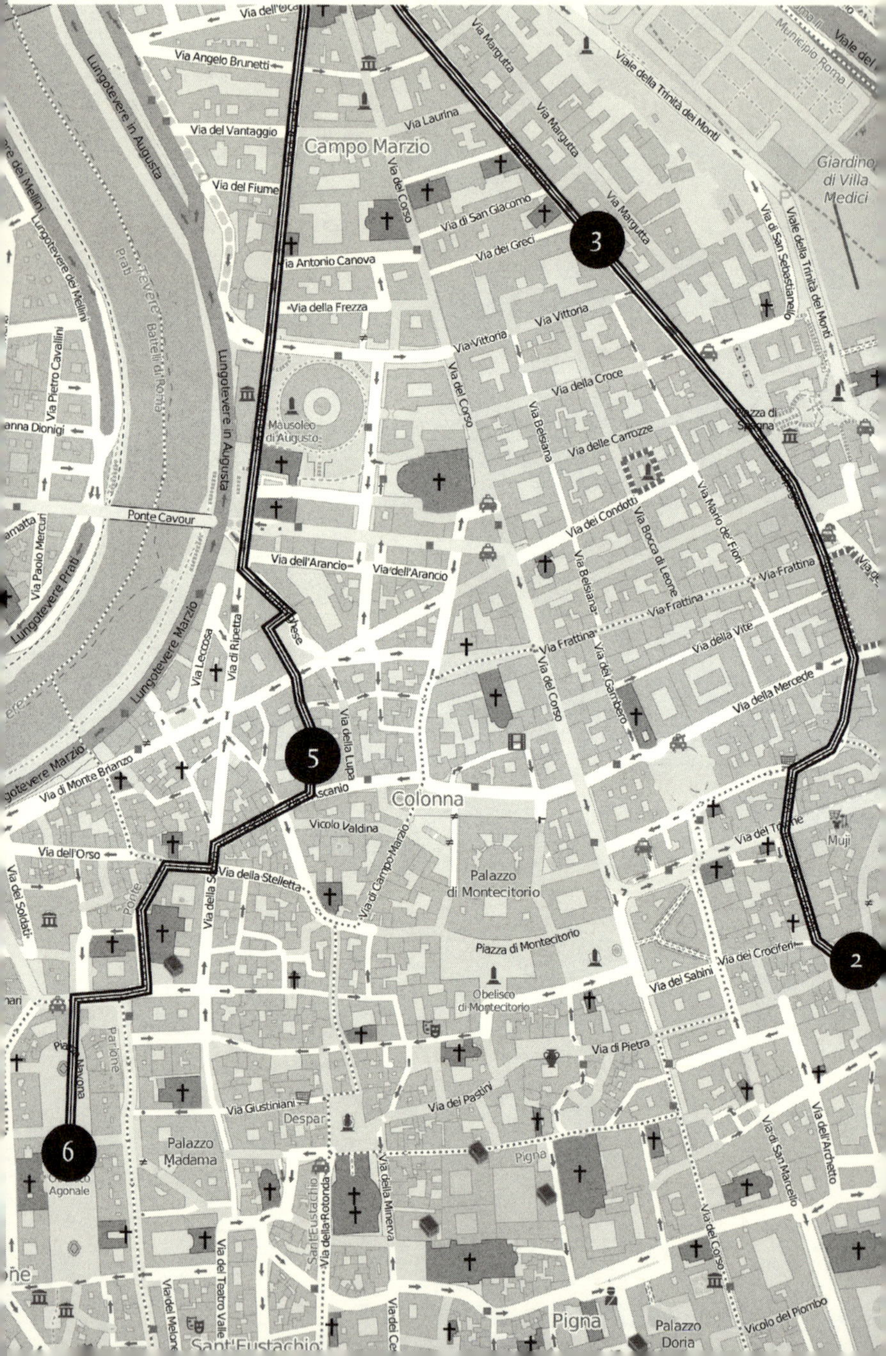

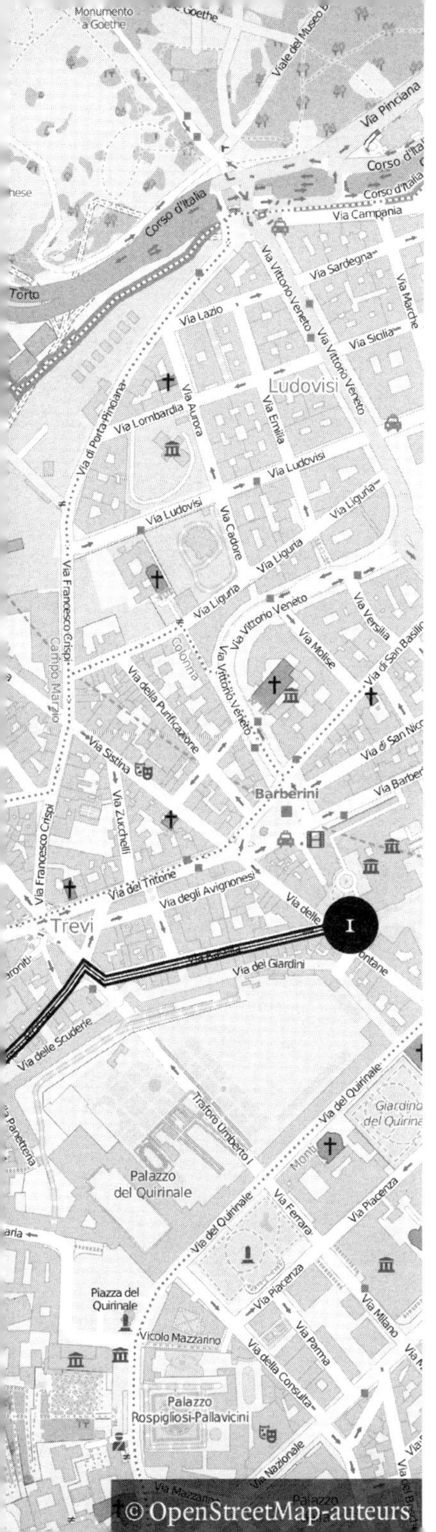

1. Via delle Quattro Fontane / XXX
2. Piazza di Trevi / XXXVII
3. Via del Babuino / XXXII
4. Piazza del Popolo / XXXVI
5. Vicolo del Divino Amore / XXV
6. Piazza Navona / XXXIII

Some sights along the way:

Trevi Fountain
Spanish Steps
Barcaccia Fountain
Piazza del Popolo
Mausoleum of Augustus
Ara Pacis Museum
Piazza Navona

Also near this route:

Piazza San Pietro (St. Peter's Square) (XXXIV)
Piazza di Spagna (XXXIX)
Via del Corso (XXV)
Via Rasella (XLVII)
Piazza Augusto Imperatore (XIII, L)

Walk 4

IN THE FOOTSTEPS OF THE GRAND TOUR AND THE BELLE ÉPOQUE

Via Muzio
Tevere
Via di Ripetta
Via Ulpiano
Via Tomacelli
Battelli di Roma
Lungotevere Marzio
Via di Ripetta
Via del Corso
Tevere
Via di Monte Brianzo
Colonna
Via dell'Orso
Via della Scrofa
3
dei Coronari
Piazza Navona
Via dei Pastini
Parione
Sant'Eustachio
Pigna
Via del Pellegrino
4

1 Piazza di Spagna / XXXIX

2 Via delle Carrozze / XXXVIII

3 Piazza Colonna / XLII

4 Piazza della Cancelleria / XL

Some sights along the way:
Spanish Steps
Column of Marcus Aurelius
Pantheon
Campo de' Fiori

Also near this route:
Piazza del Teatro di Pompeo (IX)
Piazza Sallustio (XI)
Via del Corso (XXV)
Campo de' Fiori (XXIX)
Piazza della Rotonda (XXXI)
Via del Babuino (XXXII)
Piazza Navona (XXXIII)
Via Vittorio Veneto (XLVIII)

Walk 5

IN THE FOOTSTEPS OF FASCISM AND THE SECOND WORLD WAR

1. Largo 16 Ottobre 1943 / XLVI
2. Via dei Fori Imperiali / XLIII
3. Via Rasella / XLVII
4. P. Augusto Imperatore / XIII, L

Some sights along the way:
Jewish Ghetto
Imperial Fora
Mausoleum of Augustus
Ara Pacis Museum

Also near this route:
Piazza del Teatro di Pompeo (IX)
Piazza del Campidoglio (XXVIII)
Campo de' Fiori (XXIX)
Via delle Quattro Fontane (XXX)
Via delle Carrozze (XXXVIII)
Piazza di Spagna (XXXIX)

CONCLUSION

THE PATH TO THE FUTURE

Whoever says that all you can find in Rome is some old rubble must be blind. The city is eternal but also eternally on the move. The two-thousandth anniversary of the death of the Emperor Augustus was celebrated exuberantly in 2014: spectacular laser shows on Augustus' forum attracted many spectators daily, and the emperor's residence on the Palatine Hill was made accessible to the public for the first time. The current Italian government is under pressure not only to protect but also to revalue its cultural heritage. Now, plans have been approved to rebuild the arena floor of the Colosseum, so performances can be held there.

In 2016, Pope Francis opened the Holy Door of St. Peter's Basilica, on the occasion of the "Extraordinary Jubilee of Mercy." A Holy Year is usually celebrated once every twenty-five years. Only twice before, in 1933 and in 1983, were "Extraordinary Jubilees" declared. In both years, the occasion was the commemoration of the death of Christ. Pope Francis likes to do things differently, and he was the first in history to call a thematic Jubilee. In the holy year of 2016, Rome welcomed millions of pilgrims.

Even in the twenty-first century, there are popes and emperors who are showing Rome a path to the future. The celebration of Roman anniversaries such as the days of Augustus' birth and death invariably give a boost to the city's ancient heritage. For two thousand years, Holy Years have resulted in street repairs and the widening of the streets of Rome, and the 2016 Jubilee was no exception.

But who can tell whether the streets in this book will still be there in one hundred years? The streets of Rome are always changing, following its meandering history. No matter how well I can find my way around the Eternal City now, roaming through its streets and its history will never bore me. The Miliarium Aureum ("Gold Milestone"), a pillar covered in gold on the Forum Romanum that was the intersection of all the roads extending from Rome to the vast Roman Empire, symbolizes an idea that perhaps no longer holds true in a literal sense, but still does figuratively for me: all roads lead to Rome.

SELECT BIBLIOGRAPHY

Birch, Debra. *Pilgrimage to Rome: Continuity and Change.* Woodbridge, 1998.

Blois, Luuk, and Bert Van Der Spek. *Een kennismaking met de oude wereld.* Rev. ed. Bussum, 2017.

Carandini, Andrea. *La Roma di Augusto in 100 monumenti.* Rome, 2014.

Coarelli, Filippo. *Roma.* Guida Archeologica Laterza, 2008.

Cornell, Tim. *The Beginnings of Rome: Italy and Rome from the Bronze Age to the Punic Wars [C.1000–264 BC].* New York, 1995.

Coulston, Jon, and Hazel Dodge, eds. *Ancient Rome: The Archaeology of the Eternal City.* Oxford, 2000. See especially pp. 42–60.

Couperus, Louis. *Reis-impressies.* Stichting Volledige Werken Louis Couperus. Utrecht/Antwerpen, 1990.

D'Innella, Michele, ed. *Roma. Guida d'Italia del Touring Club Italiano.* 9th ed. Milan, 1999.

Galinsky, Karl. *Augustus: Introduction to the Life of an Emperor.* Cambridge, 2012.

Hackworth Petersen, Lauren. "The Baker, His Tomb, His Wife, and Her Breadbasket: The Monument of Eurysaces in Rome." *The Art Bulletin* 85, no. 2 (2003): 230–57.

Hughes, Robert. *Rome.* London, 2011. Dutch edition: Hughes, Robert. *De zeven levens van Rome.* Translated by Frans Van Delft. Amsterdam, 2011.

Hupperts, Charles, and Elly Jans, eds. *Laus Romae. Hoofdstukken uit de geschiedenis van Rome.* Leeuwarden, 2010.

Lendering, Jona. *Stad in marmer. Gids voor het antieke Rome aan de hand van tijdgenoten.* Amsterdam, 2002.

Livy. *The Rise of Rome, Books 1–5.* Trans. T. J. Luce. Oxford World's Classics. New York, 2008.

Magistri Gregorii. *The Marvels of Rome* (*Mirabilia Urbis Romae*). Edited and translated by Francis Morgan Nichols. 2nd ed. with new introduction, gazetteer, and bibliography by Eileen Gardiner. New York, 1986.

Painter, Borden. *Mussolini's Rome: Rebuilding the Eternal City.* New York, 2005.

Stambaugh, John. *The Ancient Roman City.* Baltimore, 1988.

Stinger, Charles. *The Renaissance in Rome.* Bloomington, 1985.

Suetonius. *The Lives of the Caesars.* Translated by J. C. Rolfe. 2 vols. Loeb Classical Library. Cambridge, Mass., 1950.

Treffers, Bert. *Een hemel op aarde. Extase in de Romeinse Barok.* Nijmegen, 1995.

Van Gessel, Henk. *Pasquino. Spot en satire in Rome.* Amsterdam, 2006.

Wallace-Hadrill, Andrew. *Rome's Cultural Revolution.* Cambridge, 2008.

INDEX OF NAMES AND SIGHTS